WHAT HAPPENED TO ME
MUST NEVER HAPPEN TO YOU.

—SACHIKO YASUI

Carolrhoda Books
A division of Lerner Publishing Group, Inc.
241 First Avenue North
Minneapolis, MN 55401 USA

For reading levels and more information, look up this title at www.lernerbooks.com.

Design by Danielle Carnito.
Main body text set in Joanna MT Std 12/16. Typeface provided by Monotype.

Library of Congress Cataloging-in-Publication Data

Names: Stelson, Caren Barzelay, author.
Title: Sachiko : a Nagasaki bomb survivor's story / by Caren B. Stelson.
Description: Minneapolis : Carolrhoda Books, 2016. | Includes bibliographical references and index. |
    Audience: Grade 9 to 12.
Identifiers: LCCN 2015043908 (print) | LCCN 2016006785 (ebook) | ISBN 9781467789035 (lb : alk. paper) |
    ISBN 9781512408935 (eb pdf)
Subjects: LCSH: Yasui, Sachiko. | Atomic bomb victims—Japan—Nagasaki-shi—Biography. | Nagasaki-shi
    (Japan)—History—Bombardment, 1945. | World War, 1939–1945—Japan—Nagasaki-shi (Japan)
Classification: LCC D767.25.N3 S74 2016 (print) | LCC D767.25.N3 (ebook) | DDC 940.54/252244092—dc23

LC record available at http://lccn.loc.gov/2015043908

Manufactured in the United States of America
1-38114-19958-4/5/2016

SACHIKO

A NAGASAKI BOMB SURVIVOR'S STORY

CAREN STELSON

CAROLRHODA BOOKS / MINNEAPOLIS

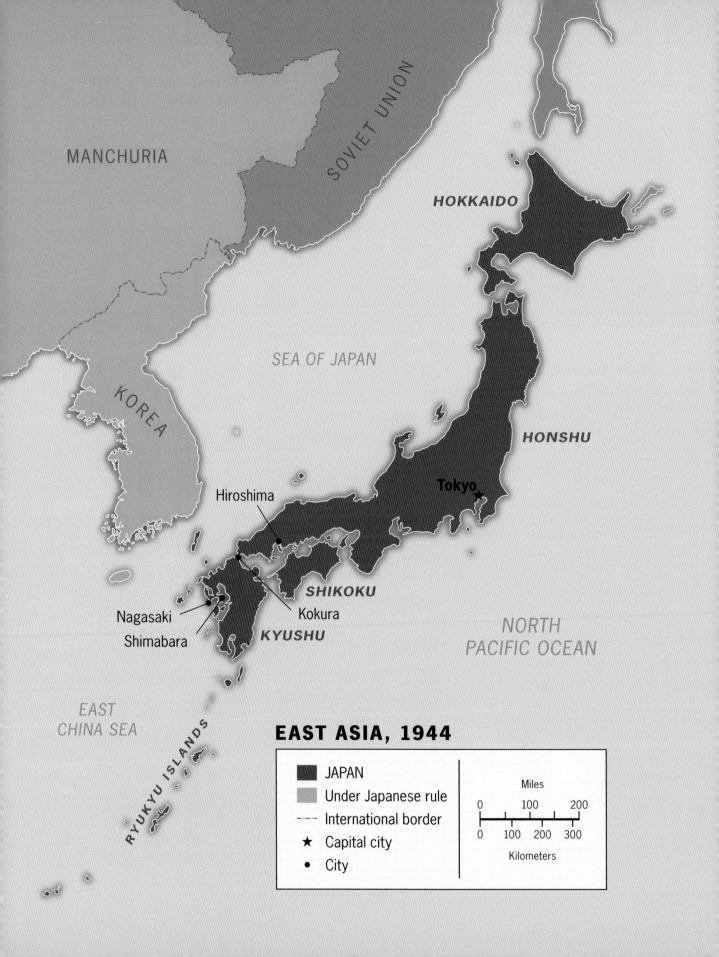

MANCHURIA

SOVIET UNION

HOKKAIDO

KOREA

SEA OF JAPAN

HONSHU

Hiroshima

Tokyo ★

SHIKOKU

Nagasaki
Shimabara

Kokura

KYUSHU

NORTH
PACIFIC OCEAN

EAST
CHINA SEA

RYUKYU ISLANDS

EAST ASIA, 1944

JAPAN
Under Japanese rule
International border
★ Capital city
● City

Miles

0   100   200

0   100   200   300

Kilometers

CONTENTS

TO KANON
花音
AND OUR NEXT GENERATION OF PEACEMAKERS

LYNDALE PARK PEACE GARDEN,
MINNEAPOLIS, MINNESOTA

PREFACE

At 8:15 a.m. on August 6, 2005, a crowd gathered at the Lyndale Park Peace Garden in Minneapolis, Minnesota. I was there with others to commemorate the end of World War II and the sixtieth anniversary of the atomic bombings of the Japanese cities of Hiroshima and Nagasaki.

A bell rang. We bowed our heads. The bell rang again. Then a speaker rose and introduced a Japanese woman to the crowd. Her name was Sachiko Yasui.

I sat in the audience motionless, listening to Sachiko tell her story about having survived the bombing of Nagasaki. I had never heard anyone share such an experience. I wondered, why didn't I know what happened to the people of Hiroshima and Nagasaki *after* the atomic bombs exploded? That day I promised myself, if ever I had the chance, somehow, in some way, I would write Sachiko's story.

In 2010 I tracked down Sachiko's address in Nagasaki and sent her a letter translated into Japanese: "We need your story in America."

Several weeks later, I received word from Sachiko. She would accept my proposal with one condition: she would tell her story only if she could look into my eyes.

Caren Stelson

SACHIKO, AGE FIVE

HOME IN NAGASAKI

AUGUST 1945

Six-year-old Sachiko sat on a worn, woven tatami mat and stared at the boiled egg in the middle of the low table.

So did her fourteen-year-old brother Aki, her twelve-year-old brother Ichiro, and her four-year-old sister Misa.

The hen had finally laid an egg.

Sachiko's stomach growled.

Mother bounced two-year-old Toshi on her lap and moved the egg closer to him. Toshi clapped his hands. The egg was his. The egg, when there was one, was always his. Toshi was the youngest.

Sachiko glanced at the egg and then smiled at her little brother. She could wait until dinnertime for her own reward. In the evening, Father would finally come home from a long day building battleships at the Koyagi shipyard. The family would be all together spending as many happy hours with Father as they could.

Steam curled out of Grandmother's bowl in the middle of the low table. Shaped as a large leaf with ruffled edges, the green ceramic bowl was Mother's treasure. Once filled with meals of squid, eel, and octopus, these days Grandmother's bowl had little to offer. Mother ladled small portions of boiled water with wheat balls into cups.

"Eat everything, children. Every drop is precious."

Sachiko sipped her boiled water. No air-raid sirens wailed. No American B-29 bombers flew overhead. Only the cicadas trilled their summer song outside the paper window.

With her last sip of boiled water, Mother hurried out to meet with the *tonarigumi,* the neighborhood association. Participation in the group was mandatory. Neighborhood leaders organized patriotic events, fire drills in case of bombings, and military training for civilians. They also distributed smaller and smaller amounts of food.

By 1945 no one in Japan had enough to eat. Families added sweet potatoes and soybeans to their near-starvation rations of rice—only two cups per month for each person. A radio broadcast suggested adding silkworm cocoons, grasshoppers, mice, snails, or the dried blood of farm animals to meals for extra protein. The government offered a recipe for flour made from powdered acorns, sweet potato vines, and mulberry leaves. The flour was barely edible.

After Mother left, Ichiro reached for his bamboo net and slipped out of the house to hunt for cicadas. Sachiko's eldest brother, Aki, took charge of the household. He watched over Misa while Sachiko played with Toshi. Sachiko tickled her little brother to make him laugh and gave him pony rides on her shoulders. Toshi was Sachiko's favorite and her responsibility.

Aki switched on the radio. Over the airwaves, a military band struck up the patriotic song "Umi Yukaba." "If I die for the Emperor, it will not be a regret," Aki sang out. He picked up his wooden kamikaze toy glider, circled it above his head, then plunged the plane straight into the tatami mat. "Umi Yukaba," he shouted. "We will win the war."

WORLD WAR II

World War II began in the late 1930s, but the roots of the conflict went back further than that. In Germany, a weak economy and a humiliating defeat in World War I (1914–1918) had created an atmosphere ripe for political extremism. Adolf Hitler rose to power in Germany in the 1930s as the leader of the Nazi Party. As Germany's dictator, he was determined to create a racially purified German empire that he called the Third Reich.

On September 1, 1939, the German army overran Poland. In response, France and Britain declared war on Germany. In June 1940, Italy's dictator Benito Mussolini sided with Hitler. War engulfed Europe. Reluctant to get involved in a European war, the United States remained neutral. But by early 1941, the United States was supporting countries fighting against the Axis powers of Germany, Italy—and Japan.

In Asia, Japan was a growing industrial power with ambitions to build an empire of its own. An island nation with limited land and natural resources, Japan looked to other Asian countries for oil, rubber, and raw materials to keep its industries and military growing. After wars with China (1894–1895) and Russia (1904–1905), Japan gained territory in Taiwan, Manchuria, and Korea.

In 1926, Emperor Hirohito came to the throne. According to national Japanese mythology, Hirohito was a sacred descendent of the gods. As emperor, Hirohito also was supreme commander of the imperial forces and head of state, although he had no official political power. The prime minister, a close circle of advisers, and the parliament governed the country. Yet as subjects of the emperor, the Japanese people were to give their complete allegiance to Hirohito. As their emperor, Hirohito was above all and held complete authority.

Emperor Hirohito, shown here in an undated photo, became emperor of Japan on December 25, 1926, at the age of twenty-five. His reign was named Showa, meaning "Enlightened Peace."

As Japan's military power increased, the nation began building its Asian empire in earnest. In 1937 the Imperial Japanese Army invaded Manchuria, attacked Shanghai, then swept into the ancient city of Nanjing. The army brutally tortured and killed hundreds of thousands of Chinese people in those cities.

Needing more oil and rubber for its warships and planes, Japan looked to colonies in Southeast Asia held by the Americans, the British, the French, and the Dutch. To limit Japan's aggression, the United States led an international ban on trade, cutting off three-quarters of Japan's imports and 90 percent of its oil supply. The ban pushed Japan into making a choice: abandon plans for an empire or risk war with the West.

The battleship USS *Arizona* after the Japanese attack on Pearl Harbor. Of the 2,335 servicemen killed in the attack, nearly half were from the USS *Arizona*. In comparison, 55 Japanese airmen died.

General Hideki Tojo became Japan's prime minister in October 1941, just two months before Japan's attack on Pearl Harbor. Known as the Razor for his quick decision making, he urged Japan to join with Germany and Italy as an Axis power. Tojo led Japan through much of the Pacific War until he was forced to resign in 1944.

Japanese prime minister Hideki Tojo, a former army general, favored war. The only force that could stop Japan's push for a larger empire was the US Pacific Fleet moored at Pearl Harbor, Hawaii, then a territory of the United States. Gambling that Americans would have little interest in a war in Asia, Tojo made a calculated decision to attack.

The morning of December 7, 1941, 353 Japanese fighter planes, bombers, and torpedo planes bombed the fleet at Pearl Harbor. Within two hours, 2,335 American servicemen were dead, more than three hundred planes were destroyed or damaged, and eight battleships demolished or badly damaged. With the Pacific Fleet crippled, Japan expected the strike would weaken Americans' will to fight. Instead, Pearl Harbor became a rallying cry for revenge.

The day after the attack, US president Franklin D. Roosevelt declared war on Japan. December 7, 1941, he said, was "a date which will live in infamy." Within three days, Allied powers led by the United States, Britain, and the Soviet Union joined together to fight the Axis powers. World War II had become a deadly global war.

The world was at war for four long years. Italy surrendered in October 1943. Germany surrendered in May 1945. Only Japan kept fighting. By the summer of 1945, as the Allies planned a massive sea invasion of Japan, US B-29 bombers were firebombing Japanese cities, one after another, with no plans to stop until Japan surrendered.

RACISM AND WAR

World War II was a conflict over power, politics, people, territory, and resources. But it was also a struggle about race, culture, and ethnicity. Under Hitler's leadership, anti-Semitism, hatred of Jewish people, fueled Germany's genocide of six million European Jews. Millions of Slavs, Roma, political prisoners, homosexuals, and others whom Hitler considered "undesirable" were killed as well. In Japan and the United States, racism also played a divisive role during the war.

Long before the bombing of Pearl Harbor, anti-Japanese sentiment existed in the United States, particularly along the Pacific Coast where many Japanese American families lived. In the late 1800s, Asian immigrants, mostly from China and Japan, arrived in the United States, providing cheap labor for agriculture, mining, and industry. As Asian immigration increased, white American prejudice toward Asians intensified. The Immigration Act of 1924 effectively ended immigration from Japan and East Asia and created an atmosphere of systematic discrimination toward Asian people.

In 1941 an estimated 127,000 people of Japanese descent lived along the Pacific coast of the United States. Many of them worked on small farms or ran their own businesses. The bombing of Pearl Harbor added fuel to the existing anti-Japanese sentiments. Fearing that Japanese families in the United States would side with Japan in the war, Roosevelt signed Executive Order 9066. The order called for the immediate imprisonment of approximately 120,000 people of Japanese ancestry in ten designated US camps. More than half of the incarcerated Japanese—62 percent—were nisei, or second-generation Japanese people, born in the United States, and therefore American citizens. With Roosevelt's executive order, discrimination against Japanese Americans became official government policy.

As the war raged on, news of brutal battles in the Pacific, torture of US soldiers in

Newspaper headlines at a newsstand in Oakland, California, in February 1942, announce the forced relocation of Japanese Americans. During World War II, "Jap" was used as a racial slur to refer to Japanese and Japanese American people.

Japanese prisoner-of-war camps, and the Bataan Death March shocked many Americans. They felt that the Japanese were a less-than-human race with an appetite for cruelty and killing. Racist American political cartoons depicted Japanese people as monkeys or rats wearing glasses and smiling with visibly large buckteeth. During World War II, most Americans viewed Germany's Hitler and his Nazis as the enemy, but hatred for Japan ran deeper. All "Japs"—emperor, soldier, or civilian, were the enemy.

In Japan, racism generated its own brand of prejudice and hate. Taking advantage of anger throughout Asia toward Western colonists, Japan called on all Asians to join together to create an Asian brotherhood. Yet in reality, Japanese military leaders intended Japan to rule over the other Asian nations. The Japanese government encouraged its people to believe in the myths of the *Yamato* race, the pure Japanese people. Those not of the Japanese race were viewed as inferior. Such beliefs emboldened Japanese soldiers to kill millions of Asians in the name of the empire.

As for white Westerners, the Japanese thought they were cowards, beasts, and monsters. "Kill the American devil," read school posters. Roosevelt and British prime minister Winston Churchill were depicted as the biggest devils of all.

Above: A US wartime poster illustrates the racist views of Americans toward the Japanese during World War II.
Below: A Japanese poster illustrates the wartime hatred for the United States, with a singular focus on US president Franklin D. Roosevelt.

EVACUATION
MAY–AUGUST 1945

Father must have known the end of the war was near.

By June 1944, when Sachiko was five, the United States had begun bombing Japanese cities with growing regularity. Nagasaki was one of the first cities bombed, although the damage was limited. In February 1945, the United States began firebombing raids over Japan's major cities, including the capital, Tokyo. After the Tokyo raid in March, one hundred thousand people had been killed, one million wounded, and one million left homeless. Then, in April 1945, Nagasaki was attacked again. Three other bombings followed, destroying shipbuilding plants along the Nagasaki harbor. Tension escalated. Japanese combat troops began moving into Kyushu, Nagasaki's home island, preparing for the US invasion that seemed sure to come.

Father made a plan to evacuate his family to a safer place. They would pack up their belongings and take the train to Shimabara, a castle town in the mountains near Nagasaki, where Father had grown up. Sachiko did not want to go. She would miss her home and her friends. Father reassured his daughter. "Sachiko, in Shimabara a house waits for you in the mountains, encircled by pines, with a lake that whispers, 'swim in me.'"

Mother filled suitcases with their worn-out clothes and family photos—of Aki and Ichiro as little boys, Mother with friends and relatives surrounded by Father's chrysanthemums from his garden, and five-year-old Sachiko wearing her red-flowered kimono. Before they left, Uncle, Mother's brother—the uncle who loved Sachiko as his own daughter—came to say good-bye. He wrapped his arms around Sachiko's narrow shoulders.

The US firebombing of Tokyo on March 9–10, 1945 *(aftermath above),* was the single most destructive bombing raid in history.

When would she see Uncle again? Sachiko asked.

No one could give her an answer.

The family returned home sooner than anyone expected.

In Shimabara, Father received his red paper, a draft notice from the government, requiring subjects of the emperor to serve in the military. With the coming US invasion, the Japanese government was drafting everyone who could fight, from boys of fifteen to men of sixty. Even unmarried women between the ages of seventeen and forty were called to serve. Father and all other soldiers would be expected to give their lives for the emperor.

Eldest brother Aki spoke first. Father should not return to Nagasaki alone. The family must leave Shimabara and go back together to make as many happy hours with Father as possible. Mother agreed. They would stay together for as long as they could until Father left for war.

Back home in Nagasaki in August 1945, Sachiko watched the sun dip below the horizon. The sky darkened. The moon rose. Sachiko, Mother, Aki, Ichiro, Misa, and Toshi stepped out onto the front porch and stared into the night, waiting for Father to come home from the shipyard. Aki held a flashlight in his hand.

In the distance, Sachiko pointed to a blink of light—Father's flashlight.

Blink. Blink—Aki's flashlight. Like fireflies longing for each other, light beams flickered and disappeared. Sachiko waited as Father trudged up the hill from the Urakami Station toward home.

Steam rose from Grandmother's bowl on the low table.

Mother ladled boiled water and wheat balls into cups.

Father, Mother, Aki, Ichiro, Misa, Toshi, and Sachiko pressed their hands together and bowed their heads.

Everyone knew that each day, each night together was precious.

SACHIKO'S FAMILY PICTURES TAKEN BEFORE 1945

ICHIRO (LEFT) AND AKI

ONE OF HER BROTHERS WITH A KAMIKAZE PILOT

MOTHER (BOTTOM LEFT) WITH FRIENDS AND RELATIVES

"PROMPT AND UTTER DESTRUCTION"

In the summer of 1945, as Sachiko's father prepared to join the Imperial Japanese Army, Hirohito listened to his advisers and generals argue.

The situation was dire. Japan had lost the air and sea wars to the Allies. Its military forces throughout its Asian empire had been defeated. Sixty-four cities on the home islands had been destroyed. More than two million Japanese soldiers and civilians had already died. How many more would perish if the Allies invaded? The options were starkly clear. Surrender unconditionally to the Americans, as they had demanded, and risk giving up the emperor's throne. Reach out to the Soviet Union, a country still neutral with Japan, and try to negotiate a conditional surrender that would keep the emperor on the throne. Or fight to the end and risk the nation's utter defeat. The emperor, the person who would decide his people's fate, remained silent.

By that summer, Roosevelt had died after suffering a massive stroke. In Washington, DC, Harry Truman was the new president. He listened as his advisers and generals debated strategies to defeat Japan. Operation Downfall, the Allied invasion of Japan, was still in the planning stage. If the invasion went ahead, it would be the largest seaborne invasion in history. Truman wanted to know how many American casualties could be expected. Perhaps thirty-one thousand dead, wounded, or missing? Probably more. No one could accurately predict the number. Would the invasion be worth the cost of so many American lives? With Japan on the verge of collapse, advisers wavered. Support for Operation Downfall began to fade.

Could the United States soften its demand for an unconditional surrender and let the emperor stay on his throne? Would that end the war? Truman's advisers argued these questions. But Truman knew the American public wanted a total and unconditional defeat of Japan.

And what of the Soviet Union? The Soviet Union had fought with the Allies against Germany but had remained neutral toward Japan. However, the Soviet leader, Joseph Stalin, had promised to go to war with Japan after Germany surrendered. Would a Soviet invasion hasten the end of the war? No doubt. But Truman didn't trust Stalin. He worried Stalin would want to control Japan and other territories in Asia after the war.

Lastly, Truman and his advisers discussed using the atomic bomb to help end the war. The bomb had recently been developed, but it had not yet been tested. Truman and his advisers hoped the upcoming test would succeed, but no one thought the atomic bomb could be an all-powerful weapon to end the war by itself.

As Truman's advisers debated, a committee formed to identify Japanese cities as potential atomic bomb targets. To demonstrate the bomb's destructive power and to terrify Japanese citizens, the target city could not have been firebombed. Yet most of Japan's cities had, indeed, been firebombed. All the same, the military identified seventeen cities as possible targets. The final list named four: Hiroshima, Kokura, Nagasaki, and Niigata.

On July 6, 1945, Truman traveled to Potsdam, Germany, to meet with the leaders of Britain and the Soviet Union to discuss Germany's surrender. At the Potsdam Conference, the Allied partnership began to fray. With Germany defeated, the Soviet Union was poised to control Eastern Europe. To Truman, the faster Japan surrendered, the less time the Soviet Union would have to interfere in Asia.

The first day of the conference, Truman received a message. The test of the atomic bomb, in New Mexico on July 16, had been successful. Truman knew that he had the most destructive weapon in human history. On July 26, the Allies issued Japan an ultimatum: "We call upon the government of Japan to proclaim now the unconditional surrender of all Japanese armed forces, and to provide proper and adequate assurances of their good faith in such action. The alternative for Japan is prompt and utter destruction."

In Tokyo the emperor remained silent.

Japanese cities bombed by the United States during the war

From left: British prime minister Winston Churchill, US president Harry Truman, and Soviet premier Joseph Stalin at the Potsdam Conference in Germany in July 1945

Truman's reply on July 30, 1945, to Secretary of War Henry Stimson approving the use of the atomic bomb

AN ORDINARY DAY

AUGUST 6, 1945

August 6 was like any other hot, humid summer day in Nagasaki. Sachiko slipped on her cloth shoes, too small for her now, and stepped into the Mezame-machi neighborhood where she lived. Sweat dampened her dark bangs and dribbled down her back. Her loose-fitting cotton *monpe* pants, tied with string at her waist and ankles, clung to the back of her skinny legs. Sachiko walked up the hill past the Sakamoto International Cemetery and trotted down the narrow road to the Sanno Shinto Shrine, toward the camphor trees. It would be cooler under the trees.

Nagasaki and its harbor in about 1920 with the Nishinaka-machi Catholic Church in the foreground.

The sun beat down on Sachiko, the Sakamoto Cemetery, the Sanno Shrine, and the ancient camphor trees. It beat on the gray-tiled roofs of the densely packed wooden houses nestled in the Urakami Valley and on the nearby Nagasaki Medical College—one of the first medical schools in Japan to teach Western medicine. It beat down on the Urakami Cathedral—the largest church in Asia—and down on the tiny island of Dejima, where trading Portuguese ships had arrived in Nagasaki four centuries ago. Open to Western trade, even when the rest of Japan was closed to the outside world, Nagasaki was Japan's pinhole where West met East.

War had turned Nagasaki into yet another Japanese city struggling to survive. Playgrounds and parks had been plowed into gardens planted with vegetables, such as sweet potatoes and pumpkins. Schoolboys carved air-raid shelters into the surrounding hillsides. To protect against raging fires ignited by firebombings, homes were taken down to make firebreaks and water tanks were constructed. And as Japan's soldiers prepared for the American invasion, schoolgirls practiced home defense with bamboo spears.

Women prepare to defend their cities with wooden spears. Every able-bodied person was expected to work for the war effort.

Sachiko was nearly to the Sanno Shrine. The massive camphor trees were just ahead. The trees were ancient, nearly five hundred years old. Their leaves, shaped like Grandmother's bowl, offered shade from the blistering sun. Beyond the camphors stood the giant, two-legged torii stone gate entrance to the Sanno Shrine. In this spiritual place, Sachiko whispered a wish—first grade.

Last April, when the air was sweet with the scent of cherry blossoms and the Japanese school year began, Father had walked Sachiko to the Zenza Primary School. She was full of excitement. "Listen to your teachers, Sachiko," Father told her. "They will guide you."

But when Sachiko and Father arrived in the schoolyard, the teachers were nervous. The American air raids had intensified. The air-raid siren shattered the morning routine that first day of school. Sachiko had just enough time to bow to her teacher before the principal sent the children home—for good. Dreams of first grade disappeared. Instead of learning to read, Sachiko learned to cover her ears and eyes with her thumbs and fingers, and if caught outside, fall flat on the ground when she heard the shout, *"Tekki!"* warning of an enemy plane.

Nights turned to nightmares.

As air-raid sirens blared, Father led his sleepy family out of the house to the air-raid cave, not far from the Sakamoto Cemetery. Grasping Ichiro's hand, Sachiko ran through the wet grass. Her protective, padded-cotton hood covered her head. Around her neck was a pouch filled with hard biscuits that bounced on her heaving chest.

At the cave's entrance, Sachiko ducked through the small opening and squatted in the dark. The chill from a soggy straw mat seeped through her cloth shoes. American B-29 engines rumbled above the cave. Inside, mosquitoes whined over Sachiko's head.

The rumbling of bombers continued. Shadowy outlines of neighbors shifted. Sachiko clenched her teeth. Misa whimpered next to Aki. Toshi sniffled on Mother's lap. Sachiko reached into the pouch and handed Misa and Toshi each a biscuit to nibble.

Minutes passed.

The rumbling of the B-29 engine turned to a drone. Then echoes. Then silence.

A siren reverberated from the city's loudspeakers. All clear.

Eldest brother Aki looked to Father and Mother. Sachiko reached for Ichiro's hand.

For now, it was safe to go home.

August 6, 1945, ended an ordinary day of war for the people of Nagasaki. Not so for the people of Hiroshima. The morning of August 6, an atomic bomb exploded over their city.

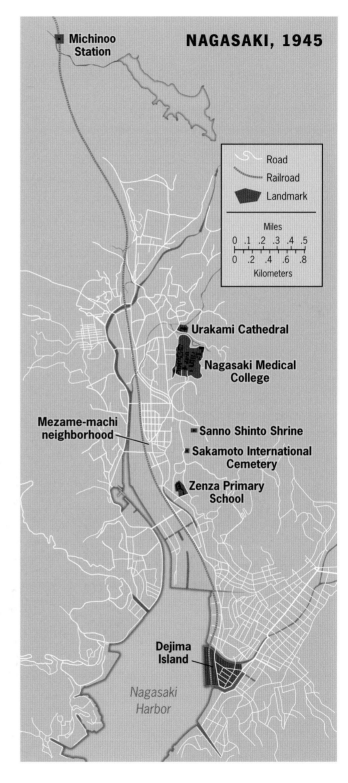

NAGASAKI, 1945

Michinoo Station

Road
Railroad
Landmark

Miles
0 .1 .2 .3 .4 .5
0 .2 .4 .6 .8
Kilometers

Urakami Cathedral

Nagasaki Medical College

Mezame-machi neighborhood

Sanno Shinto Shrine

Sakamoto International Cemetery

Zenza Primary School

Dejima Island

Nagasaki Harbor

LITTLE BOY AND FAT MAN

On August 6, 1945, at 2:45 a.m., Lieutenant Colonel Paul Tibbets sat in the cockpit of the B-29 bomber the *Enola Gay*, named for his mother. Tibbets and the other pilots chosen to fly the atomic bomb missions over Japan had been practicing for more than a year.

Two planes that would accompany the *Enola Gay* had taken off earlier that morning, one to photograph the explosion and the other to collect scientific data. After receiving a signal, the *Enola Gay* lifted off the runway of the tiny Pacific island of Tinian, 1,567 miles (2,522 kilometers) southeast of its target city, Hiroshima. In the bomb bay was a 9,700-pound (4.4-metric-ton) uranium atomic bomb code-named Little Boy.

At 8:09 a.m., the *Enola Gay* flew undetected over the coastal city of Hiroshima. From the air, Hiroshima was an ideal target. With a wartime population of about 340,000, it was a major city. And it had never been bombed. Houses, schools, stores, and military installations were still standing. The people of Hiroshima went about their morning routine under a cloudless sky. At 8:14 a.m., the *Enola Gay*'s bombardier sighted the city's Aioi Bridge over the Ota River. The bombardier then pressed the automatic control switch, and the doors to the bomb bay opened.

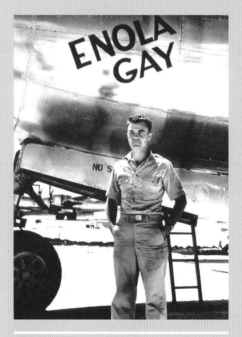

Lieutenant Colonel Paul Tibbets in front of the *Enola Gay*, the B-29 he piloted over Hiroshima on August 6, 1945

Little Boy hurled downward, nose first, toward Hiroshima. At 1,900 feet (580 meters) above the city, the gun mechanism inside the bomb case fired, setting off an unstoppable nuclear chain reaction. Little Boy exploded with a force equivalent to 15,000 tons (13,600 metric tons) of TNT (trinitrotoluene), releasing deadly radiation into the air and sending shock waves in all directions.

The heat from the flash measured more than 1,800,000°F (1,000,000°C), hotter than the surface of the sun. At the hypocenter, the point on the ground immediately below the explosion, temperatures reached between 5,432°F and 7,232°F (3,000°C and 4,000°C). Every living thing within one-third of a mile (500 m) of the hypocenter was charred to death. Within ten minutes, an atomic cloud mushroomed and rose 60,000 feet (18,290 m) into the air, drawing soil, debris, and dust particles with it. The particles, now radioactive, flew through the air as deadly fallout or as black rain.

The morning bombing of August 6, 1945, left 92 percent of Hiroshima destroyed and approximately seventy thousand people killed. The number of dead doubled in the months to follow as wounds, burns, and radiation sickness killed additional people.

Rumors of the explosion reached Tokyo. Unsure what to do, the emperor stalled.

The same day, Truman announced the atomic bombing of Hiroshima to the American public saying, "If [Japan's leaders] do not now accept our terms, they may expect a rain of ruin from the air, the like of which has never been seen on this earth."

Three days later, in the early hours of August 9, 1945, Major Charles Sweeney sat in the cockpit of the B-29 bomber *Bockscar*. Resting in the bomb bay was a plutonium atomic bomb code-named Fat Man with an explosive force of 21,000 tons (19,050 metric tons) of TNT.

Sweeney was ready for takeoff. His prime target was the industrial city of Kokura. If for any reason the Kokura mission failed, the next city on the list would be Nagasaki.

As *Bockscar* flew toward southern Japan, the Soviet Union began an invasion of Japanese-controlled Manchuria, as Stalin had promised. Neither the people of Nagasaki nor most Americans knew what was happening.

Military engineers carefully assemble Fat Man, the plutonium nuclear bomb, on Tinian Island in August 1945. The code name Fat Man is said to refer to British prime minister Churchill. The Hiroshima bomb's code name Little Boy is a reference to US president Roosevelt.

Twenty-five-year-old Major Charles Sweeney in the cockpit of *Bockscar*, the B-29 bomber that dropped the atomic bomb on Nagasaki

UNSPEAKABLE SECONDS

AUGUST 9, 1945

Sachiko rolled off her futon and rubbed her eyes. Already, cicadas were
buzzing outside the paper window. Father had left early for the harbor to visit
a sick friend. Mother was in the kitchen, patting wheat balls in the palms of
her hands. Mother seemed jumpy, nervous.

Had anyone found the egg?

No?

Strange?

Two-year-old Toshi pointed with his tiny finger. Look, he said, dancing
from foot to foot.

The hen had sauntered into the house, clucking and pecking. Toshi
squatted, glanced at Mother, and pointed again. He laughed out loud, his eyes
full of mischief. The hen hadn't taken off her shoes!

Sachiko glanced at the hen's clawed feet. Hens in shoes? Toshi could be
so silly.

Mother did not laugh. She chased the hen out into the garden.

Still no egg?

Mother tightened her cotton kimono around her waist and carefully
dished out breakfast from Grandmother's bowl. "Come, children. Eat quickly."

7:50 a.m.

A rumble drowned out the trills of cicadas. Mother looked up.

The air-raid siren blared, growing louder, longer, higher, arching into
a wail.

"Hurry, children." Mother gathered up Toshi.

Sachiko ran for her padded hood. Aki helped Misa find hers. Ichiro grabbed Sachiko's hand.

The siren pulsed.

The family fled, running to the air-raid cave. Sachiko ducked into the cave's entrance and sat on a soggy mat. In the gray shadows, she could make out the outlines of children from the neighborhood, four of them, three girls and a boy.

8:30 a.m.

The air-raid siren stopped.

The all clear sounded.

Everyone in the cave stood and stretched. Mother held Toshi's hand and left the cave to search for the hen's egg. Ichiro ran to hunt cicadas with a friend. Aki and Misa walked home to listen to the war news on the radio.

The oldest of the children in the cave, a ten-year-old girl, stepped up to Sachiko. "Do you want to play house with us?"

Play house? Of course, Sachiko wanted to play.

"I'm the oldest," the ten-year-old shouted out. "I'll be the mother."

Sachiko sat with the three girls and the boy on an old rush mat near the emergency water tank, a collection of broken roof tiles in front of them. They pretended roof tiles were plates. Mud balls were dirt dumplings. Sachiko laughed, putting her small hand over her mouth. She patted her mud dumpling and seasoned it with grass.

The late morning sun rose higher in the sky.

Cicadas hummed.

Clouds billowed.

9:45 a.m.

Captain Sweeney flew B-29 *Bockscar* over the city of Kokura with the atomic bomb Fat Man secure in the bomb bay. After Hiroshima, Kokura was the next city on the list of atomic bomb targets. The winds began to shift. Thick clouds rolled in. *Bockscar*'s crew could not see Kokura through the clouds.

Sweeney circled Kokura a second time. Japanese antiaircraft guns began firing. Sweeney circled the city a third time. The bomber's crew grew nervous. The fuel pump had not been working properly on takeoff that morning. They were flying with less fuel than expected, and time was running out.

Sweeney calculated *Bockscar*'s fuel consumption. The bomber still had enough fuel to fly over the next target on the list—Nagasaki. The crew could drop the atomic bomb and then radio for an emergency landing. Sweeney turned the bomber toward the city.

A few seconds after 11:00 a.m., *Bockscar* began its descent. Nagasaki too was impossible to see. Cumulous clouds covered the city.

Above the clouds, the engine whined.

Sachiko sat on the rush mat patting her mud dumplings.

The ten-year-old "mother" cocked her head and listened.

A US B-29 Superfortress bomber over Nakajima Aircraft Company, Musashino Plant, Japan. The *Enola Gay* and *Bockscar* were stripped of all guns except the tail gun to accommodate the weight of the atomic bombs they carried in their bomb bays.

Bockscar's crew squinted down. Their aiming point was the Mitsubishi shipyard along the harbor, but they couldn't see it. Suddenly a cloud parted, briefly revealing Nagasaki's densely populated Urakami Valley, 1 mile (1.6 km) off target. The bombardier looked down through the hole in the cloud. "I got it! I got it," he yelled out. He squinted, took aim, and released a switch. The bomb bay opened.

Fat Man hurled toward the city.

11:01 a.m.

The ten-year-old froze.

"Tekki!" she yelled out.

Sachiko threw herself facedown on the mat, covered her ears, and squeezed her eyes shut. Was this pretend?

11:02 a.m.

PIKADON!

THE END OF THE WORLD

AUGUST 9, 1945

An eerie, blinding light burst in the sky. Red, blues, greens spiraled. Hot, deafening, hurricane-force winds roared, and at the center of the explosion, a giant fireball flamed, hotter than the surface of the sun.

The earth shuddered.

Sachiko shot up into the air.

She slammed down into the ground.

Stones, tiles, branches, leaves rained on top of her. Piled up. Pushed her down. Buried her. Dirt poured into her nose and mouth.

Sachiko lay quivering 900 meters, just over half a mile, from the hypocenter.

The force of the winds snapped electrical wires, mangled streetcars, blew out windows, yanked doors off hinges, toppled houses, and hurled pieces of glass like bullets. The Nagasaki Medical College was gutted. The Urakami Cathedral collapsed. The Sanno Shrine crumpled. Roaring winds ripped the bark off the camphor trees and split their trunks. Scorched black by the flash, the camphors stood naked, their roots clinging to the earth. The heavy stone torii gate stood unsteadily on one blackened leg. The singing cicadas vanished.

Above Nagasaki, a vertical atomic cloud formed, 2 miles (3.2 km) overhead, swirling into the shape of an enormous mushroom.

Fires ignited everywhere. Roof tiles blistered. Melting lampposts twisted like taffy. Smoldering rubble rubbed out roads. Whole streets vanished.

Writhing, roiling, the cloud climbed higher and higher into the sky, as if it were alive.

Then, as the mushroom cloud covered the sky, its top folded, smothering the sun like a thick, gray blanket.

Dust erased the lines of the earth.

Day turned to night.

Sachiko could not move. Pinned under the rubble, she could hear the muffled voices of her friends calling out, "Mother. Mother, help me."

THE NAGASAKI
ATOMIC BLAST
AS SEEN FROM
KOYAGI

Sachiko tried to call out too, but her mouth, nose, ears, and throat were so clogged with dirt and ash that she couldn't make a sound. Something pressed on the back of her neck and under her chin. She could barely breathe.

She was choking.

How long she lay trembling under the mound of rubble, Sachiko did not know. Then hands grabbed her ankles. Fingers pressed into her skin. The strong hands yanked her legs, but her head remained lodged under something heavy across the back of her neck.

Again, the fingers pressed into her skin. The hands pulled.

Little by little, Sachiko's stomach scraped over dirt, leaves, and tree bark. Her chin bumped against stones. The hands moved from ankles to hips, grabbing her waist, throwing her up and out onto the ground. Sachiko's head throbbed, her throat ached. Dirt burned under her eyelids. In front of her, a tall shape spun in a dizzy whirl. The face came into focus.

Uncle.

"Sachiko!" Uncle held her by the shoulders.

"Sachiko," Mother screamed, her eyes wild, her face smudged with sweat and soot. "Sachiko, are the other children here too?"

Sachiko tried to answer, but she couldn't breathe.

Uncle turned her around and whacked her between her shoulder blades. Sachiko sputtered, coughed, caught her breath.

Gasped.

The city had turned to ash.

All around, not a house, not a tree stood. Not a leaf, stem, or blade of grass remained. Bits of paper fell from the sky.

Uncle wasted no time. He turned his hands into shovels and dug Sachiko's playmates out of the earth. One by one, four limp children lay side by side on their backs, their mouths filled with dirt.

Dead. All of them.

Dazed, dizzy, Sachiko buried her face in Mother's torn kimono.

Uncle disappeared and came back with Misa in his arms. He had found her sitting on the ground staring into space, seemingly unhurt. Mother held Misa close.

But where was Aki? And Ichiro?

Where was little Toshi?

There was no time to search.

Smoke and the hot, acrid smell of burning rubber filled the air. Flames like snake tongues licked telephone poles, consumed flattened houses, gobbled anything in their path. The fire was coming closer. Everywhere people were streaming away from the burning city and toward the safety of the mountains.

"Follow me," Uncle shouted. He hoisted Misa onto his shoulders. Both Mother and Uncle lifted the dead children into their arms. They picked their way through the Sakamoto Cemetery, up the path to the mountains.

Uncle led the way.

Sachiko followed, barefoot. The blast had blown off her shoes. Coughing from dirt and smoke, she climbed over rocks, stumbling, crying, feeling nothing except the heat of the earth on the bare soles of her feet.

Everyone was dirty, thirsty, exhausted. Uncle settled Mother, Sachiko, Misa, and the dead playmates on the hillside. Sweat ran down Sachiko's face.

"Where was Toshi? Where was he?" Mother cried, tears staining her cheeks. She had left Toshi in the garden, running after the hen.

"Wait here." Uncle hurried down the path.

Mother, Misa, and Sachiko sat numb, staring at the earth below, as it turned red with fire.

A shout rang out.

Aki?

Yes, Aki. The boy stood shaking before Mother, explaining how he had pulled himself out of the wreckage when the house collapsed around him, how he had wandered through the Sakamoto Cemetery until he had found them. No, he hadn't seen Ichiro or Uncle. No, not Toshi either. Aki winced with pain. Through Aki's ripped shirt, Sachiko could see his right shoulder and his upper back. Both were raw with burns.

Another familiar voice shouted out.

Ichiro stumbled toward them, his cicada net still in his hand.

Aki. Now Ichiro. A miracle.

Ichiro's eyes were crazed with fear. Hunting cicadas, Ichiro's friend had been killed right in front of him, struck in the head by sharp, flying debris. Ichiro had raced home, looking for everyone, but the house had collapsed. No one was in sight.

Mother, Sachiko, Misa, Aki, and Ichiro sat together, quaking, waiting for Uncle's return. From the hillside, people shouted the names of sisters, brothers, mothers, and fathers. Desperate to flee, people crawled on hands and knees, their hair frizzled by flames. Some, their backs blackened with burns. Some, their faces swollen like pumpkins. Some, their arms stretched in front of them, skin hanging in shreds, moaning, *"Tasukete kudasai"* (Please help me).

What had happened?

No one knew.

Uncle appeared.

Sachiko flinched.

Mother covered her open mouth with her hand.

Uncle stood rigid, holding little Toshi in his arms, a wooden stick piercing the boy's head.

Mother reached for her dead son and pressed his soft, sooty cheek next to hers.

Dust mixed with twilight.

Hours passed.

Then another familiar voice shouted. Father's.

Another miracle, how else to explain it?

Father had been visiting a sick friend near the harbor. As soon as he could after the explosion, he had picked his way home. The 3-mile (4.8 km) walk from the harbor had taken hours. Father caught his breath, then stared at little Toshi in Mother's arms.

Fire crackled.

The hills filled with the wounded.

Father pulled his gaze away from Mother and Toshi. He turned to Uncle. They could not stay here. They would have to turn back to the Sakamoto Cemetery. They would be safer there. After that, Father and Uncle would decide what to do.

Sachiko glanced at her playmates' bodies. That morning they had been playing house.

MIZU

AUGUST 9–11, 1945

The gravestones in the Sakamoto Cemetery had been hurled out of the earth by the force of the bomb, leaving large holes in the ground.

Sachiko huddled in a hole beside Mother. The stones around them, once gray, had turned orange from the intense heat. Below, fires flared.

Feeble voices pleaded, "*Mizu. Mizu.*" (Water. Water.)

Sachiko was thirsty too. So thirsty. But there was no water.

Sachiko crept closer to Mother—Mother who still held the body of little Toshi. A chill ran through Sachiko. She leaned into Mother for warmth.

Rain began to fall.

Mizu. Mizu. Water. Water.

The raindrops were not clean and clear but strangely dark and oily. The rain stained Sachiko's clothes, splattered on her bare arms. She tried to wipe off the greasy drops, but they only smeared on her skin.

More hours passed. B-29 bombers continued to rumble overhead. Bright fires continued to burn. Moaning echoed over the hillside. Father and Uncle came to the same conclusion. They could not stay at the cemetery. Everyone needed clean water—and food. They must head to a safer place. But Sachiko, huddling cold and wet in her hole, could not think of food. Fire, smoke, fear, and dread had sucked away her hunger.

Dawn's light appeared without notice.

Suddenly the bombers disappeared. The sky quieted. Only the sound of buzzing flies remained.

The buzzing grew louder.

Flies were everywhere.

———

By twilight, Father and Uncle had made a plan: return to Shimabara.

Father had heard rumors that rescue trains were running at Michinoo Station, taking people away from the city. If Sachiko's family could get to Shimabara, they could find help.

Mother sat on the ground, holding Toshi in her stiff arms. "No." She shook her head. No, she would not go. She would not leave her baby son here by himself.

Father looked into Mother's eyes. Of course. They would bury Toshi as properly as they could. Sachiko's playmates too. Uncle nodded and turned to retrieve the four little bodies they had left on the hillside.

A child with her mother in Nagasaki on the morning of August 10, receiving rice dumplings from emergency supplies. The child is wearing a cotton air-raid hood.

Together, Father, Mother, Aki, Ichiro, Misa, and Sachiko began to carve out shallow graves with shards of tile sharp enough to dig into the dirt, lump by lump. To dig took all Sachiko's strength, digging and shooing away the flies.

Uncle returned, struggling as he carried the four small bodies to their graves.

Mother pressed Toshi to her chest. "Forgive me," she whispered, laying Toshi in a shallow trench in the earth. "Forgive me. I could do nothing to save you." Mother crossed Toshi's arms over his chest.

Toshi dead? Her little brother, her *ototo*. Sachiko could hardly believe she would never again hear Toshi's small hands clap or see his shining eyes.

Father scooped up a fistful of soil.

"Stop, I can't bear it," Mother cried out. She ripped a piece of fabric from her kimono with her teeth and twisted the strip around her finger. Gently she cleaned Toshi's eyes and nose of mud, then spread the ragged cloth over the little boy's head. "At least the soil will not touch his beautiful face." When they had finished burying him, Mother placed a stone marker on Toshi's grave.

———

Dusk seeped into the day.

The evening sky deepened to night.

All during the night, Sachiko sat in her cemetery hole, her throat dry, her lips cracked, listening to voices crying for water.

Mizu. Kudasai. Water. Please.

"Sachiko." Father bent over her, touching her shoulder. "It's time to go. Follow me. Remember, never lose sight of me. Do you understand?"

Sachiko held Mother's hand. Misa clung to Mother's back. Aki walked with Father. Ichiro followed Uncle.

The station and the rescue train were nearly 3 miles (4.8 km) away.

Ichiro struggled to keep up. He could not stop vomiting. Father urged him on. Aki cried out in pain. His shoulder was so badly burned that he could hardly walk. Father bent over and eased his eldest son onto his back.

Sachiko tightened her hand around Mother's warm fingers.

Mother followed Father in a trance, one foot in front of the other.

People searching the bombed areas of Nagasaki for family members and their homes

Everywhere everything was burned, bent, mangled, destroyed. Factories. Homes. Schools. Shrines. Temples. In the dark, shadowy telephone wires hung low. Uprooted trees cast their silhouettes across the landscape. In the distance, their roots looked like splintered broomsticks.

One step, another step, Sachiko walked on through hot ash, her arm over her nose, trying not to gag. Fires raged, and the air filled with the stench of burned bodies. Flames lit up outlines of horses, charred like lumps of coal. Human bodies lay in the road like stones. Some dead. Some alive.

Ashes burned Sachiko's bare feet. Father bent down to collect ragged strips of cloth fluttering on the ground, blown from kimonos, shirts, pants. He stopped, eased Aki off his back and stooped next to Sachiko. Gently, Father wound strips of cloth around her tender feet.

Murmurs swirled as Sachiko walked on.

Mizu. Kudasai. Water. Please.

Desperate voices whispered, "I can't bear it anymore. Kill me. Kill me."

Sachiko stumbled. Her foot hit something hard—no soft. A body. Two bodies. A mother and a baby, burned. Sachiko could not move.

"Sachiko." Father's voice broke through her fear. "Sachiko. Think nothing. Nothing. Just follow me."

Sachiko stepped over the bodies. Over another. Another. Over outstretched legs. Over outstretched arms.

Mouths whispered, "Water, water, water."

The sun rose as Sachiko and her family reached the train station and joined a crowd of survivors on the platform. Except for her brothers and sister, Sachiko had not seen another living child. Still, there was Aki, Ichiro, and Misa. She had Mother, Father, and Uncle. They huddled together on the platform, all dying for water.

"ENDURING THE UNENDURABLE"

AUGUST 12–15, 1945

Sachiko watched as steel and steam emerged along the tracks. A rescue train appeared out of the smoke. Doors opened. Father lifted Sachiko inside. Wounded bodies filled every seat, every space.

Shoulder to shoulder, chin to chin, Sachiko inched her way through the crowded train car. Father, Mother, Aki, Ichiro, Misa, and Uncle sat folded together. Sachiko could hardly breathe.

The train jerked forward.

No food.

No water.

The train chugged along the tracks and stopped at the next station.

Wounded bodies pressed against the train doors. To get into the cars, survivors on the platform slid down the train windows and squeezed through.

The train lurched forward again.

Aki's shoulder flared. Ichiro spiked a fever. Misa was listless.

Sachiko's throat burned. She wanted water to drink more than air to breathe.

"You must resist," Father said. "We must sip on hope that we will arrive in Shimabara alive."

One day.

Two days.

Three days.

Four.

Many tram stations in Nagasaki were destroyed.

As the rescue train chugged toward Shimabara, the emperor's Supreme War Leadership Council bickered over the terms of surrender. What would happen to Japan? As the council delayed a decision, American B-29 bombers continued their firebombing. With sixty-six Japanese cities now destroyed, there was not much left to bomb.

August 15.

The rescue train chugged into the Shimabara Station. Relief workers took the injured off the train in stretchers and lined them up on the platform like fish in a market.

At noon an unfamiliar recorded voice spoke over the radio. It was the emperor. People were stunned. Never before had the Japanese people heard their emperor speak. Hirohito delivered his message using official language. "The war situation has developed not necessarily to Japan's advantage . . . we have resolved to pave the way for a grand peace for all generations to come by enduring the unendurable and suffering what is insufferable."

An announcer followed, rereading the emperor's message in easier language. "We had no choice but to lay down our arms."

Everywhere in the station, in the streets, people looked bewildered. Some fell to their knees. Some cried. Some prayed.

Japanese people weep as they listen to the broadcast of Hirohito announcing Japan's surrender on August 15, 1945.

The war was over.

Over.

Japan had surrendered unconditionally. The US military would occupy the nation. After two thousand years, Japan would face for the very first time an occupying enemy on its own soil.

Who knew what horrors might come next?

TWO BROTHERS

Sachiko's family huddled together at Shimabara Station. What should they do? Aki writhed in pain. His burned shoulder and back were red with infection, oozing and throbbing. He needed a doctor, medicine, a hospital.

And Ichiro. What was happening to Ichiro?

Father leaned into his younger son and spoke softly. "Ichiro, you have survived all this way from Nagasaki to here. Stand up."

But Ichiro could not stand. He felt dizzy, faint, hot. His temperature was spiking. His hair was falling out in clumps. His gums bled. Ichiro needed a hospital as badly as his older brother.

The hospital in Shimabara was tiny. Only six worn futon mats covered the floor, all of them occupied, except for one. Both Aki and Ichiro needed the empty futon, but as each hour passed, Ichiro needed the futon more.

Uncle agreed to take Aki and Misa to stay with Father's relatives. Mother, Father, and Sachiko would stay with Ichiro on the hospital floor to help him and ease his pain, if they could.

The few doctors and nurses at the hospital worked mechanically throughout the day, spreading their meager supply of ointment, Mercurochrome, or sometimes vegetable oil on wounds and burns. Ichiro had no open wounds, yet his illness grew worse. He was unable to eat and could not drink. Small purple spots spread over his body.

"How is it possible for such a strong, healthy boy to become so sick?" Mother asked. If she only understood what was wrong, she could take care of her son. She should know how to care for her children, she thought. As

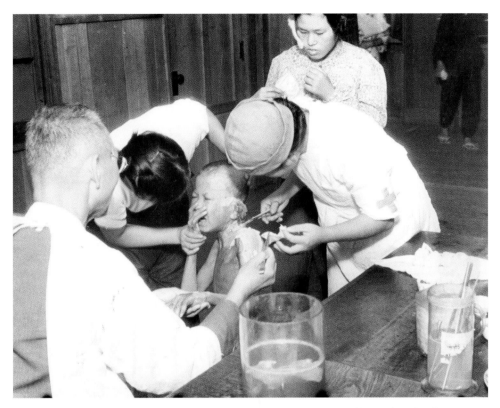

A small child receives treatment at a makeshift hospital set up in a Nagasaki school.

parents, they had always relied upon the knowledge of the past.

Father shook his head, "The past is useless now."

On August 24, Ichiro lay limp on the hospital futon near delirium. Ichiro—the brother who always took care of Sachiko—was now too sick to hold her hand.

Father turned to Sachiko and shouted. "Hurry, go to the nurse."

Sachiko ran for help. She returned with only a small cup of water. Her hands trembled so much that she spilled some of the water down her front. She put the cup to her brother's lips, but Ichiro could not drink.

A nurse brought ice chips in a bowl and placed a cooling piece on Ichiro's tongue.

"Sachiko." Ichiro reached for her hand. "Sachan, take care of everyone."

Sachiko wanted to shout to her brother, but words stuck in her throat.

Father grasped Sachiko's hand and placed her palm on top of her brother's. "Take care of everyone." Ichiro whispered for the last time.

Sachiko stared at her dead brother, her *onisan*.

"Ichiro! Ichiro. Come back."

Father and Mother returned to the house to see Uncle and Misa and to bring Aki back for medical treatment. At the hospital, one futon lay vacant on the floor. Mother and Father gently lowered Aki to the mattress. He winced, then gazed around the room. "Where is Ichiro?"

"Ichiro is struggling to survive," Father lied. He eased next to Aki. "So are you. You are the eldest son. Listen. The person who survives puts all his strength together to live. You need not escape this world. The war is over."

Aki's eyes widened. "What did you say, Father?"

"The war is over," Father repeated.

Aki swallowed, mustering words. "What was the result?"

"We are defeated."

A Nagasaki atomic bomb survivor rests on a mat.

"What?" Aki struggled to sit up. "We lost the war?"

Sachiko looked from brother to Father.

"Yes, we lost." Father's voice went quiet. "Japan lost the war."

"How can that be?" Aki stared at Father, trembling, fighting feverish tears. "Everyone said we were winning. Japan was winning."

Father sat in silence, covering his face with his hands.

"Father, why are you crying?" Aki licked his dry lips. "I don't believe Japan lost. Father, please wipe your tears. Please, for our Japanese brothers, wipe your tears. We will fight until we win. Father, sing 'Umi Yukaba.'"

Sachiko's chest clutched under her dirty blouse.

Aki slumped back on the futon, exhausted. "Please, Father, sing as if I were a kamikaze pilot. Sing, 'If I Go to the Sea.'"

Aki closed his eyes and mouthed the words as Father sang with a choked throat,

> *If I go to the sea,*
> *I shall be a corpse washed up.*
> *If I go to the mountain,*
> *I shall be a corpse in the grass.*
> *But if I die for the Emperor,*
> *It will not be a regret.*

Eldest brother Aki, Sachiko's *onisan*, stopped breathing.

Father's shoulders shook, and his head swayed in his hands. Sachiko couldn't say a word. Words had turned to ash in her heart.

MIRACLE

Days slipped by.

More sad news came.

Uncle died. Sachiko's *ojisan.*

His throat had become so inflamed that he could not eat or drink. The uncle who had saved Sachiko was gone. More sad news from Nagasaki arrived too. Twenty-three of Mother's relatives were dead.

Sachiko, Misa, Mother, and Father struggled to survive in their Shimabara house surrounded by pines with the lake that had once called to Sachiko, "swim in me." But Sachiko was too ill to hear the lake calling. Instead, she heard her dead brothers. In Sachiko's delirium, Aki, Ichiro, and Toshi came to her, smiling, reaching out, wanting to play.

Sachiko lay in bed, hovering between life and death. She was too ill to eat, too tired to concentrate. She spiked a high fever. Her hair fell out. Her gums bled. Tiny purple spots appeared on her body, spread, and within a few days grew into dots the size of peas. Lesions opened in her skin. Flies laid eggs in them. The maggots caused itching and excruciating pain.

Sachiko's dead brothers called to her again, "Come with us."

Father and Mother fell ill too. So did Misa. Wrapped in an old, borrowed blanket, Sachiko and Misa leaned against each other, listless.

The fall rains came. Lightening flashed. Thunder rumbled. In Sachiko's nightmares, bombers flew overhead. In the middle of the night, she screamed, waking Misa next to her. Mother held her two small daughters close and cried with them.

suffered from radiation sickness, which few at the time understood. People who were exposed to the radiation often showed few or no signs of illness at first. The symptoms came in stages. Thirst, weakness, nausea, fever, diarrhea, and vomiting were the first signs of radiation sickness. Three to six weeks later, more symptoms appeared: hair loss; bleeding gums; listlessness; and a prolonged, elevated fever of 104°F (40°C). Purple spots dotted the skin, indicating internal bleeding. Painful sores in the mouth and throat were also common, making swallowing difficult. Infections often set in, further weakening a person's condition and leading to delirium and death—or to a long, painful recovery.

The scientists who had developed the atomic bomb were unaware of the effects of full-body radiation exposure. They had not conducted any tests on the potential impact of radiation on humans. Nor had the US military tried to develop medical treatment for radiation exposure before the bombs were dropped. Doctors offered what treatments they could. Radiation sickness would continue to perplex doctors in the months and years to come.

Nagasaki's geography affected the extent of damage in different areas of the city. Mountains helped contain the blast's destruction and the spread of radiation.

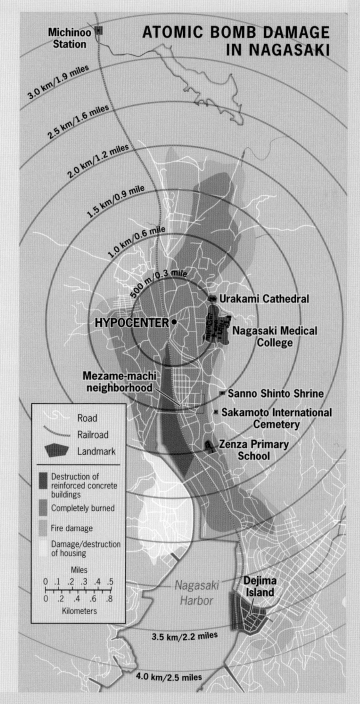

ATOMIC BOMB DAMAGE IN NAGASAKI

Michinoo Station

3.0 km/1.9 miles
2.5 km/1.6 miles
2.0 km/1.2 miles
1.5 km/0.9 mile
1.0 km/0.6 mile
500 m/0.3 mile

HYPOCENTER •

Urakami Cathedral

Nagasaki Medical College

Mezame-machi neighborhood

Sanno Shinto Shrine

Sakamoto International Cemetery

Zenza Primary School

Road
Railroad
Landmark

Destruction of reinforced concrete buildings
Completely burned
Fire damage
Damage/destruction of housing

Miles
0 .1 .2 .3 .4 .5
0 .2 .4 .6 .8
Kilometers

Nagasaki Harbor

Dejima Island

3.5 km/2.2 miles

4.0 km/2.5 miles

A NEW BEGINNING

SPRING 1946

Seven-year-old Sachiko leaned her head against the train window as the landscape slipped by. The mountains of Shimabara faded in the distance. Father, Mother, Misa, and Sachiko were on their way back to Nagasaki. Father had explained the only direction was forward. The four of them must return, revive their lives, and begin again. And Father would take Sachiko to school. He promised.

Three small white boxes filled with ashes traveled with them on the train. Uncle. Aki. Ichiro. What would home be like without them? Without Toshi.

The train chugged into Nagasaki Station. Much of the city was still ash. Nearly everything in the 1.5-mile (2.4 km) area around where the atomic bomb had exploded had burned and collapsed. Eighty thousand people had been left homeless. Instead of tile-roofed houses of wood and paper, makeshift shacks dotted the hillside. Dirty mats flapped against window openings and on poles jutting out from entrances to air-raid caves. Father, Mother, Misa, and Sachiko were not the only people searching for new beginnings. Japan itself—weary of war and wary of what would happen next—was on the threshold of a new beginning.

Sachiko's new beginning would take place on the island of Koyagi, where Father had worked in the shipyards before the atomic bombing. Since Father could take his old job there, he had decided that Koyagi was where the family would start again.

A harbor island, Koyagi was about 10 miles (16 km) from Sachiko's old neighborhood. It was on the other side of the mountain ridge that ran through the city of Nagasaki. When the atomic bomb exploded, the ridge had served as a protective wall. Those living in Koyagi were saved from direct radiation exposure and injury. Buildings and schools still stood.

Sachiko's new home was in a two-story cement apartment building that the shipbuilding company provided. With no electricity or running water, each small apartment had little more than a floor and a roof. The window offered a view of the glittering mouth of the Nagasaki harbor.

Mother found a wooden crate for the apartment and draped a white cloth over it. On it she placed the three small boxes filled with the ashes of Aki, Ichiro, and Uncle.

Sachiko pressed her hands together and bowed.

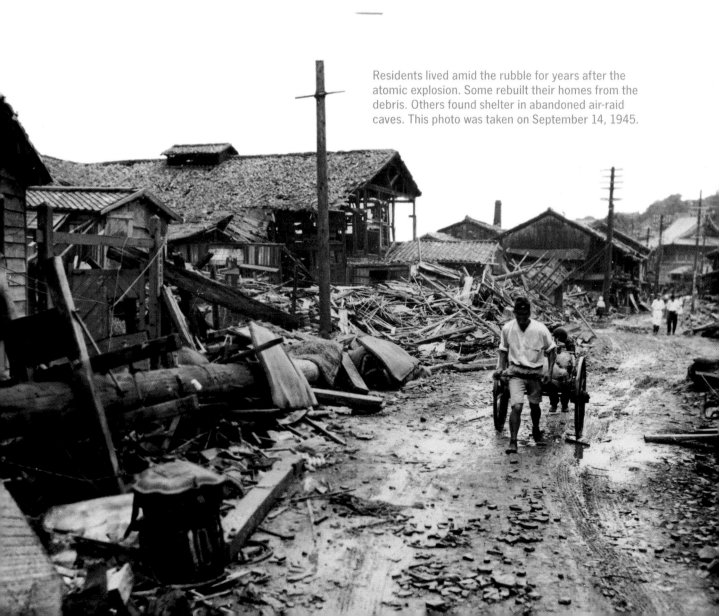

Residents lived amid the rubble for years after the atomic explosion. Some rebuilt their homes from the debris. Others found shelter in abandoned air-raid caves. This photo was taken on September 14, 1945.

"Stay away from the soldiers," Father reminded Sachiko as she ventured outside to explore her new neighborhood.

Articles had appeared in the *Nagasaki Shimbun,* the city's newspaper, with warnings about American soldiers who had come to occupy Japan:

> *Women, stay on your guard! Men, also stay indoors on the day [of their arrival]. . . . When alone, avoid direct contact with the foreign soldiers. If the other party approaches you and speaks, do not panic, do not smile, especially women and children, and do not answer them in clumsy English.*

The children didn't listen to the warnings. They gathered in groups in the streets, shouting out "Good morning" to the long-legged Americans.

"*Ohayo. Ohayo,*" the children shouted in Japanese.

American soldiers in Sasebo, a major naval base for the Japanese located north of Nagasaki. The writing on the left side of the poster says, "Enforce salute rigidly." The writing on the right says, "Keep discipline strictly."

"Ohio?" a soldier would say. "Oh heck, I'm from Indiana." The soldier would slap his knee and smile, showing his white teeth.

"*Haro, haro,*" the children would say, trying out their best hellos.

Sachiko hung back in the crowd, peeking from behind a utility pole. She did not shout like the others. She observed.

Ichiro, look at them, she said to her brother in her mind.

Ichiro, you would never imagine such strange people like these soldiers. They are so tall. And their hair. Red, yellow, brown.

Sachiko stepped a little closer.

And their eyes are strange too—green, brown, gray, blue, and so round.

A smiling soldier crouched, one knee on the ground. He reached into his pocket. Would he pull out a gun? No, Sachiko knew that American soldiers had no weapons. When the soldier pulled his hand out of his pocket, small squares wrapped in paper appeared in his palm.

"*Haro. Haro,*" the children shouted.

The soldier beckoned the children with his finger to come closer, then tossed the squares in the air.

Sachiko, like a shy kitten, took a step and caught one.

Still smiling, the soldier held up a papered square, slowly unwrapped it, and popped it into his mouth. He ran his tongue along his lips and smiled some more.

The crowd of children unwrapped their squares and popped them into their mouths too.

Sachiko slowly picked at the paper until it pulled apart. Inside was something dark and brown. She placed the square on her tongue. A sugary sensation exploded in her mouth. Saliva flowed. A hot jolt ran through her body. She swallowed and licked her lips. Although she had eaten, it was the first time since the atomic bomb that Sachiko had tasted anything.

What is it? Brother Ichiro asked in Sachiko's imagination.

Chokoreto. Chocolate.

Delicious.

American soldiers might not be devils after all.

THE US OCCUPATION

With the US occupation of Japan after the war, the Japanese people faced sweeping changes, starting on the day of Japan's official surrender.

On the morning of September 2, 1945, the battleship USS *Missouri* and 260 other Allied ships clogged Tokyo Bay. On the deck of the USS *Missouri* were US general Douglas MacArthur, the Supreme Commander of the Allied Powers (SCAP), representatives from nine other Allied countries, and Japanese officials. Hundreds of sailors looked on as Japan officially surrendered. Allied and Japanese representatives signed the Instrument of Surrender. In twenty-three minutes, the Pacific War had ended. One person was noticeably absent from the ceremony—Hirohito.

As the head of the US occupation of Japan, MacArthur took charge of Japan. More than 240,000 American troops entered the country to enforce the occupation. They met no resistance. Soldiers, particularly those assigned to Hiroshima and Nagasaki, were shocked by the devastating conditions. In letters and diaries, they wrote of the eerie silence, the mangled metal from streetlamps and factories, the smell of rot, and the hunger and despair on people's faces.

The destruction of Japan was nearly impossible to calculate. By some accounts, out of a population of 74 million in 1941, 2.7 million Japanese servicemen and civilians died during the war. This was almost 4 percent of Japan's people. Another 4.5 million soldiers who returned home were sick, starving, or wounded.

MacArthur began the task of transforming Japan so that Japan would never again threaten the United States. He started by completely disarming the Japanese nation, taking away all weapons of war. Pro-military Japanese government ministers were ousted or tried for torture and other war crimes they had set

General Yoshijiro Umezu, chief of the Imperial Japanese Army general staff, signs the surrender document on the USS *Missouri,* with General MacArthur *(behind microphone)* watching at Tokyo Bay on September 2, 1945.

in motion. Shintoism was abolished as the state religion. New reforms made it possible for farmers to own their own land. New trade unions encouraged workers to bargain for better conditions. Women gained the right to vote.

Yet the occupiers were often undemocratic. For example, MacArthur and a committee of American officials wrote a new constitution for Japan. Article 9 of this new constitution stripped Japan of its ability to make war:

1. *Aspiring sincerely to an international peace based on justice and order, the Japanese people forever renounce war as a sovereign right of the nation and the threat or use of force as means of settling international disputes.*
2. *In order to accomplish the aim of the preceding paragraph, land, sea, and air forces, as well as other war potential will never be maintained. The right of belligerency of the state will not be recognized.*

This famous photo was taken on September 27, 1945, during the first meeting between General MacArthur and Emperor Hirohito. The photo was published in the Japanese newspapers to the amazement of the Japanese people. At one glance, the photo established MacArthur's authority as supreme commander of occupied Japan.

Other actions by MacArthur contradicted the spirit of democracy. The new constitution guaranteed freedom of expression, but in practice, the heavy hand of censorship banned articles, reports, passages in school textbooks, movies, or any text that questioned General Headquarters authority or informed the public about the war or the atomic bomb.

One of MacArthur's most controversial decisions was to keep Hirohito on his throne but to take away his power. This action prevented war crimes courts from trying the emperor as a war criminal. Hirohito would have his throne, but he would no longer be viewed as a god and supreme ruler of the nation. Instead, MacArthur would rule Japan.

SCHOOL

Father kept his promise to take Sachiko to school. He had already made arrangements with the principal.

Sachiko was all nerves and excitement getting ready. School would be like chocolate. She would meet other children in second grade. She would learn to read, write, add, and subtract. She had missed first grade because of the war, it was true, but that shouldn't matter. In her mind, she promised to tell brother Ichiro everything.

The April breeze brushed Sachiko's cheeks. Father held her hand as they walked to the Koyagi schoolyard for the first day of the school year. "Listen to your teachers, Sachiko," Father said. "Remember, your teachers will guide you."

The first stop was the school's office. The principal surveyed Sachiko up and down. She felt his eyes on her patchy scalp where hair had yet to grow back. Her scaly skin. Her fragile body. Her clothes, worn out and too small. Her secondhand shoes.

The principal shook his head, glancing at Father, then back to Sachiko. "You've had a horrible experience. It *would* be wiser if you started over in first grade."

First grade?

The principal's words felt like a slap.

"No!" The word shot out of Sachiko's mouth before she could stop it. "No," she said again, stomping her foot. "Why not second?"

Father's eyes were full of surprise. "Sachiko, why do you say such a thing?"

The principal glanced at Father. "It's impossible," the principal whispered. "I doubt if she can even write her name."

"No," Sachiko said again. The word was powerful. If she went backward, what would brother Ichiro say in her dreams? She needed to go forward.

"No," Sachiko repeated. "If I start in first grade, I won't go to school."

The principal pondered his answer. "All right. I'll let Sachan enter second grade but on one condition." The principal caught Father's eye. "If she cannot catch up, she will be placed back in first."

———

Sachiko sat at her second-grade desk with her lunch box close by. Inside was a bun made from corn powder and baked sweet potato that Mother had prepared for her. Sachiko let her gaze swivel around the room, taking in the details. Compared to her new home, the classroom felt like a palace, with glass windows, wooden desks, chairs—and books.

Sachiko's second-grade textbook lay in front of her. Now that the American military occupied the country, Japanese schools had new rules. Schools were required to remove the emperor's portrait from the wall. Teachers were also told to have their students draw black lines with brush and ink through any references to the emperor and the Japanese military in their old textbooks. Children also learned a new vocabulary. Three words were the most important—*freedom, democracy,* and *peace.*

But *freedom* and *peace* are more than words in a textbook. Out on the playground, children who had survived the bomb were often teased. The name-calling stung. Bullies hurled out words such as *baldy, monster* or, worse, *tempura*—referring to the Japanese style of deep-fried vegetables, fish, and other food.

With full heads of hair, wearing socks and shoes, Sachiko's classmates stared at her.

"Why do you wear the same ugly clothes every day?"

"Why is your neck so dirty?"

"Don't you ever wash your hair?"

"How come you can't read?"

"How come you can't even add 2 + 3?"

"Are you stupid? Lazy?"

One child stole her lunches.

Sachiko hated school.

At night, brother Ichiro came to her in her dreams. His words echoed in her mind, "Take care of everyone."

How could she?

Every day after school, Sachiko ran home, crying. She could not find the words to tell Mother about the teasing—the bullying—how much it hurt to be picked on for things that could not be helped. How could she explain her dizziness? Her inability to stand during the morning assemblies. Her lack of concentration. Her loneliness. Her envy of other children's laughter. She had no words to describe her anguish.

Besides, Mother had her own struggles.

So did Father.

And Misa.

"Why can't you understand anything?" Sachiko's teacher tapped her fingers on her desk. "Tell me, why?" Even the teacher couldn't make sense of Sachiko's behavior.

Nagasaki's Chinzei Middle School was destroyed by the atomic blast. The school was about 0.4 miles (600 m) from the hypocenter. The Urakami district had eleven schools within 0.6 miles (1 km) of the Urakami Cathedral, and all were destroyed or severely damaged.

In truth, how could the teacher understand what Sachiko had been through? Under US occupation, the government strictly enforced censorship. No word was to seep out about the sickening and often deadly effects of radiation on the human body. Censorship agents carefully reviewed newspapers, magazines, movies, books, and scientific studies. Any criticism of, information about, or photos of the use and impact of the atomic bomb were deleted or blackened out. Even the Japanese characters for *genshi bakudan,* "atomic bomb," could not be printed.

Through her tears, Sachiko called to her brother in the clouds. *Ichiro. Help me.*

"If you have enough energy to cry every time you come home from school, then you have energy to use your words," Mother said one day after school. She handed Sachiko a metal rod. Together they went outside and sat in the dirt.

With Mother's help, Sachiko pressed the rod's tip into the ground. A vertical line. A curve. Then a horizontal line. Each character of each word had to be carefully drawn. Together, they spelled her name, Sachiko.

Mother rubbed out the characters with her foot. "Again, Sachiko," she said.

Every day, Sachiko practiced in the dirt. Over and over. Stroke by stroke. Until the sun went down. Until she could no longer see. She practiced through the weeks, through the months.

At the end of the school year, the principal summoned Sachiko to his office. Sachiko bowed low. The principal reached for a piece of paper on his desk saying, "Show this to your mother and father." He handed her the paper, the words written in fine calligraphy. This was a Certificate of Excellence for mastering the curriculum in second grade.

Sachiko raced home, her treasure grasped in her hand. Mother greeted her with a smile, the first smile Sachiko remembered her mother offering since the bomb. Together they stood in front of the overturned wooden crate with the three small boxes on top that served as the family's altar. Mother placed the certificate at the base of the middle box.

Sachiko pressed her hands together and bowed her head.

Ichiro, it's me Sachan.

Look, Brother, I did it!

SEARCHING FOR HOPE

DECEMBER 1947

Eight-year-old Sachiko had just finished third grade in Koyagi when Father announced it was time to move again. The move could not be helped. With little work at the shipyard, Father had lost his job. Mother packed the three small white boxes of ashes, the wooden crate that served as the family altar, and their few belongings. They would return to the site where their small house with paper windows had once stood near the Sakamoto Cemetery, the Sanno Shrine, and Sachiko's beloved camphor trees.

Nagasaki had begun to rebuild. The sound of pounding hammers and saws reverberated throughout the city. Calls of encouragement rang out, "Well done." "Keep up the fine work."

In the Urakami Valley where the atomic bomb had detonated, buildings and utility poles were slowly emerging out of the dust. Streets reappeared. New streetcars replaced mangled ones. Schools reopened. Huts became homes. Nagasaki was still filled with blowing dust and rubble. But much of the remaining radiation—from the fallout that polluted the air, water, and soil after the atomic bomb exploded—had scattered, decayed, or been washed away by rains.

After the atomic bombing, a rumor had spread that nothing in Hiroshima or Nagasaki would grow for seventy years. But flowers *had* bloomed. The graceful limbs of oleander trees, full of pink blossoms, swayed in the breeze. Morning glories sent their tendrils up fence posts. Sweet potatoes, wheat, and corn sprouted. Earthworms moving through the soil gave people hope.

Yet, despite the new growth, people still silently worried about the bomb's effects. The morning glory flowers were smaller than usual, and sometimes their leaves were deformed. Sweet potato plants sprouted but often with no crop.

Sachiko's mother and father worried about six-year-old Misa. Ever since the bomb, she had been weak and ill, with no energy to go to school. As Sachiko, Mother, and Father found their way back to their old neighborhood, Misa struggled to keep up.

The destruction from the bomb was still evident. At the Sanno Shrine, the large stone torii gate that marked the entrance still stood on one leg. The other leg, amputated in the bomb blast, lay cracked and broken on the ground.

The five-hundred-year-old camphor trees were still suffering too. The blast had blown holes through their ancient trunks. At the bottom of the holes, dust and debris lay in layers. The trees themselves stood upright, tall, holding tight to their roots. Pungent waxy leaves had sprouted along their outstretched branches, and white blossoms peeked out.

Nagasaki's One-Legged Torii Gate stands near the Sanno Shrine among the atomic ruins. A camphor tree, stripped of its bark, is in the background.

Mother gazed up at the giant trees and clapped her hands. "Well done, camphors," she applauded. "You have not only survived—you are growing."

Sachiko gazed up too. Mother was right about the trees. But could Sachiko be as strong as the camphors?

The family traced their way back to the area where their house had once stood. Father began to dig in the ashes. Sachiko picked through the rubble, collecting nails, tiles, and pieces of scorched wood. A Buddhist monk, a friend of Father's, offered timbers from a demolished shrine. Father would use these materials to build their new home.

"Look here! Look what I found," Father shouted. He dropped his shovel; fell to his knees; and used his hands to push aside broken roof tiles, chunks of cement, and splinters of wood. Gently he tugged out something green, shaped as a leaf. It shimmered in the sun.

Grandmother's bowl.

The bowl had survived without a crack or chip. Father handed the bowl to Mother.

Tears stained Mother's cheeks like raindrops. Slowly, she brought the bowl to her chest. Her treasure. Everyone's fingerprints—Uncle, Aki, Ichiro, and Toshi—were on that bowl. Alive or in spirit, they were all together again.

Grandmother's bowl

Mother found a special place for Grandmother's bowl in the new house—or rather, the new shack. There was little room for much more than Grandmother's bowl, Father, Mother, Sachiko, and Misa. With its dirt floor and two stones for a kitchen fire, the shack was like many others that clung to the hillside. The roof leaked when it rained. The wind found holes in the walls and howled through them.

For dinner, Mother cooked sweet potato leaves, wild grass, or whatever else she could find that was edible. She made meals over a fire, in a pan pulled out of the rubble. She poured water from an earthen jar with a broken neck and served the day's meals in Grandmother's gleaming bowl.

Father, Mother, Sachiko, and Misa ate from Grandmother's bowl, washed their faces in Grandmother's bowl, rinsed their clothes in Grandmother's bowl. When the sun disappeared and the sky grew dark, Father and Mother set Grandmother's bowl aside and prepared for bed. To sleep, they leaned against opposite walls, crossed their arms, and stretched out their legs, their toes nearly touching the other side of the room. The family had no mats or futons. Sachiko and Misa curled up with their parents, laying their heads on their parents' thighs. Misa's head on Mother's. Sachiko's on Father's. The four slept tangled and connected until the morning sun rose overhead.

A SEED FOR THE FUTURE

FEBRUARY 1, 1948

"This is the only world we can live in, Sachiko. Never say evil words, otherwise we'll not see peace. Hate only produces hate." These were the words Father said to Sachiko, the words he lived by.

Each day Father walked to the public library to study and read the newspaper. Each day he returned home to share whatever he had learned.

One afternoon in early February, nine-year-old Sachiko found Father outside, shoveling rubble to make space for a new chrysanthemum garden. The news weighed heavily on him. Father put his hand on Sachiko's shoulder. "The world has lost a great man."

Sachiko was confused by Father's words, but she could read his troubled eyes.

The great man Father was speaking of was India's Mohandas K. Gandhi, or the Mahatma, as the world knew him. Newspapers around the world reported that on

In 1930 Gandhi led thousands in a march to the sea to protest the British colonial tax on salt. The Salt March and Gandhi became known throughout the world.

January 30, 1948, Gandhi had been killed by an assassin's bullet. News articles reminded people of Gandhi's leadership to help win India's independence from British rule without firing a shot and of his philosophy of peace and nonviolence. "Nonviolence is the greatest force at the disposal of mankind," were the words Gandhi lived by.

Father had studied Gandhi and his philosophy of nonviolence. His hand still lay on Sachiko's shoulder. "You are too young to read Gandhi's works, but one day you must study Gandhi. You will learn something you will need for the rest of your life."

Sachiko did not understand the meaning of Father's words, but the serious tone of his voice made a great impression.

Hate only produces hate. Father's words echoed in Sachiko's mind. She studied Father as he wrapped a tiny bandage around the leg of a wounded mouse, invited a stray cat and dog to live with them in their shack-house, dug a pond for a goldfish, and made a garden out of rubble. Father had seen enough war. He was trying to build a peaceful world for his daughters to live in.

Sachiko listened to Father's advice and planted Gandhi's name in her mind, although she didn't know quite why.

STANDING UP TO
THE BULLIES
APRIL 1948

"Listen to your teachers. Remember, your teachers will guide you," Father reminded Sachiko again as she prepared for her new fourth-grade class in her old neighborhood.

The school building in Sachiko's Mezame-machi neighborhood had been mostly rebuilt, but the playground was still full of broken glass, cement, and rubble. As Sachiko peeked inside her classroom, the teacher invited her in. He turned to his students. "Please welcome Sachiko as a friend from Koyagi."

Sachiko slipped behind her wooden desk, hoping she would recognize a friend or two. No one looked familiar. Why would they? Sachiko had been one of the very few children in her neighborhood who had survived the bomb.

Sachiko turned her attention from her classmates to the front of the room. During math class, the teacher pointed to arithmetic problems on the board. Sachiko raised her hand. Each time the teacher called on her, Sachiko's answer was correct.

At lunch, a strange mood fell over one of the girls in Sachiko's class, one who seemed to be the leader of a gang. Sachiko flashed back to her experience of being taunted at school in Koyagi. What was it this time? Didn't the girl like Sachiko's clothes? Her hair?

Outside on the playground, the girl made it clear. She didn't like Sachiko's intelligence. And she was not happy that the other girls in her gang wanted to get to know Sachiko. Out on the playground, the girl began to bully Sachiko. Threaten her. "Watch out, I have two older brothers," the girl warned.

Two brothers?

The taunt ripped open Sachiko's heart. Aki, Ichiro, *her* two older brothers would have come to her rescue. Grief washed over her like a tsunami. After school, Sachiko ran home, spilling hot tears.

"Sachiko," Mother pulled her daughter close. "Look at me. Since the bomb, you have not found your mind." Mother rose and searched for a scarce sheet of paper and a pencil. "Write what is in your mind, Sachiko. You haven't explained your mind since it happened. Sit down. Make a composition. Write."

Sachiko did not want to write. She had no interest in writing.

"Write," Mother said.

Sachiko's memories were a jumble. Write? How would she ever begin?

She stepped outside and sat on a rock next to the shack. There was more light outside. More space. More quiet. Where should she start?

With the egg?

She could start with the egg.

Little Toshi always got the egg. But that day, the hen had not laid one.

Sachiko willed herself to remember more.

The air-raid siren that morning. The all clear. Her friends who asked her to play house. How she loved playing house.

The laughter.

The mud dumplings.

Then the whining coming from the clouds.

Her friend shouting, "Tekki!"

The flash.

Sachiko at about twelve years old, sitting on what she called her "study rock" near the shack where she lived with her family

Pikadon!

Sachiko let the memories of the atomic bomb explode in her mind.

The horror. The heat. The smell. The fear. Little Toshi.

Aki.

Ichiro.

Ichiro. Ichiro.

Sachiko began to write. She wrote until her hand hurt, until the pain in her heart subsided, until her mind cleared.

The next day at school, Sachiko handed her teacher the composition, as Mother had urged. The teacher read Sachiko's story word for word quickly to himself. His breath slowed. "So this is what happened to you, Sachiko?"

The moment stretched in the silence.

"Why not publish this in the school newspaper for your classmates?"

The day the next school newspaper was printed, the students read Sachiko's story silently to themselves, word for word.

Sachiko would remember that day.

That day the bullying stopped.

As the month of August approached, the atmosphere of Nagasaki was heavy with memories of the atomic bombing. City officials were preparing a commemorative service for the third anniversary of the bombing, to honor the dead and give hope to the living. *Aki, Ichiro, and Toshi.* Sachiko had written their story for school, but what else could she do to honor her dead brothers?

The morning of August 9, Mother brought home a bag of ice chips. Mother had decided the family would *not* go to the commemoration. Instead, Sachiko, Misa, and Father gathered around Grandmother's bowl as Mother filled it with the ice. Accepting a piece of ice on his feverish tongue was the last thing brother Ichiro had been able to do. From now on, this is how the family would remember the morning of August 9, 1945.

In the city, a crowd gathered at the hypocenter.

11:02 a.m.

The city of Nagasaki fell silent.

The crowd bowed their heads over their hands.

Father, Mother, Sachiko, and Misa bowed theirs over Grandmother's bowl.

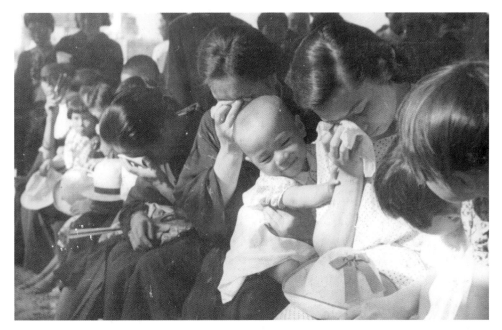

People in Hiroshima gather to pray on August 6, 1946—the first anniversary of the atomic bombing of their city.

The crowd at the hypocenter whispered the names of their dead and tried to forgive. Try to forgive whom? Themselves? One another? Forgive all those who had survived for not being able to save all those who had perished? The guilt of surviving the atomic bomb weighed as heavily on the minds of the living as their grief.

Never again. Never again. The words from the crowd repeated like drumbeats.

At home, Mother wept.

"The war is over," Father said as Mother cried. "What if we had had another disaster? What if we had had another war? Can you imagine? No, the war is over. It is good. It is good."

Sachiko clung to Father's words.

ANOTHER SEED FOR THE FUTURE

OCTOBER 1948

During the autumn of 1948, excitement spread through Nagasaki after an announcement appeared in the newspaper. On October 16, an important person would arrive at the city's train station. Father must have known who was coming, but Sachiko decided to find out for herself.

After school, with permission, Sachiko and some friends headed for the Nagasaki Train Station. A large number of people had already gathered. More arrived. The crowd swelled from five hundred to five thousand. Sachiko squeezed through spaces, between bodies, avoiding elbows, pressing closer to the platform for a better view.

A train chugged down the track.

Sachiko stood on her tiptoes.

The mayor of the city waited on the platform with a few children and a group of city officials, forming a greeting party. They turned their heads as the train approached.

The crowd suddenly erupted in applause.

A tall woman with graying hair and a brilliant smile stepped off the train. She wore a Western-style dress, sandals, and a hat. Sachiko stared. The stranger was beautiful. The woman walked across the platform with deliberate high steps, her hat tilted on her head. Her round eyes looked like those of the American soldiers'.

Another round-eyed woman wearing Western dress accompanied the smiling stranger. The two women seemed to be friends. Their fingertips danced in the palms of each other's hands.

The stranger with the brilliant smile smiled even more.

Again, the crowd erupted, this time singing a Japanese song Sachiko did not know.

> *Happy little bluebird.*
> *Flew to Japan . . .*
> *All the way from a foreign country*
> *To this country. To this town.*
> *The bird flew to Japan, over the sea.*
> *The little bird always stays on Helen Keller's shoulder.*

Helen Keller?

The stranger was Helen Keller?

Helen Keller smiled at the crowd, her blue eyes unfocused, her face full of happiness. She hummed along with the crowd, keeping the beat of the music with her fingers.

Helen Keller traveled to the city of Kobe in 1948 on her way to Nagasaki. Known throughout Japan, Helen Keller *(left)* was greeted by crowds in each city she visited. Polly Thomson *(right)* traveled with Keller.

Sachiko watched, mesmerized.

When the singing ended, Helen stepped behind a microphone. Her round-eyed friend, introduced as Miss Polly Thomson, stood at Helen's side. Helen cleared her throat and spoke to the thousands before her in a breathy voice, slowly, without changing pitch, sometimes garbled, but with great determination. Sachiko could see that.

The friend repeated out loud what Helen Keller said. A city official standing with them translated into Japanese: "May Nagasaki surrounded by the beautiful sea, be rebuilt to an even more beautiful city than it was before it was so damaged."

Two of the children in the greeting party, students from a school for the deaf and blind, stepped forward and presented Helen Keller with a bouquet of flowers. Helen Keller kissed the children. *"Arigato."*

Arigato? Helen Keller knew the Japanese word for "thank you"?

The women walked off the platform and stepped into a waiting car. *"Sayonara,"* Helen called out as she waved good-bye under a blue, blue sky.

Helen Keller. Sachiko would have to ask Father more about her.

Of course Father knew of Helen Keller. She was famous throughout Japan, even before her travels began. Her autobiography *The Story of My Life* had been translated into Japanese. Writer, peace activist, and tireless worker for the disabled, Helen Keller had come on a mission to Japan—her second—to help her blind friend Takeo Iwahashi raise donations for the deaf and blind. As almost everyone knew, Helen Keller herself was deaf and blind.

Deaf? Blind? That afternoon, Helen Keller had stood in front of thousands at

Polly Thomson *(left)* became Helen Keller's companion after Helen's teacher Anne Sullivan died in 1936. Helen with Polly traveled widely advocating for people with disabilities. This photo was taken in about 1950.

the Nagasaki Train Station, smiling, singing, and speaking into a microphone. Sachiko had loved Helen Keller's spirit and the saucy way her hat tilted on her head. Helen Keller—the first American woman Sachiko had ever seen with her own eyes—how could Helen Keller be deaf and blind?

Helen Keller's childhood was legendary. As a toddler, Helen had suffered a terrible illness, possibly scarlet fever, that had left her in a dark, silent, frustrating world. The day Anne Sullivan arrived was a new beginning for Helen. Anne Sullivan, or Teacher, as Helen called her, endured tantrum-filled days before she could calm the rage and fear of her young student and spell words into Helen's hand. Communicating in sign language was a way for Helen to live beyond her darkness. But by the age of ten, Helen wanted to speak with the power of her own voice.

Anne found Helen a speech teacher who could help. With sensitive fingertips, Helen practiced feeling the physical formation of words—the movement of the tongue and throat, the breathing from the nose, the vibrations on the lips. Helen learned first to vocalize, then utter sounds, words, sentences, entire thoughts. It mattered little if Helen's speech was garbled. She learned to speak her mind.

The autumn of 1948, Helen Keller spoke with her own voice to the people of Hiroshima and Nagasaki. Touching the scars from burns on people's faces both sickened Helen and filled her with indignation. The trip to Hiroshima and Nagasaki "scorched a deep scar" on her heart, Helen later wrote. "I felt sure that I smelt the dust from the burning of Nagasaki—the smoke of death." As Helen Keller left Japan, she resolved to fight "against the demons of atomic warfare . . . and for peace."

Sachiko would not forget the day Helen Keller came to Nagasaki. Helen reminded Sachiko of the camphor trees, strong and determined. Here was a woman who surmounted her own disabilities, found light in darkness, hope in despair. With her outstretched arms, Helen Keller showed it was possible to embrace the world.

Sachiko planted the image of Helen Keller in her mind and placed it beside the memory of Gandhi.

She would need them both.

MISA AND THE ORPHANS OF WAR

1949–1954

Damage from the war and the atomic bomb blast was all around Sachiko, even as another war in the Pacific brewed. The simmering conflict was in Korea, only 150 miles (240 km) from Nagasaki, across the Korean Strait.

Father was alarmed by the prospect of another war as his family struggled to rebuild their lives out of the rubble. But in 1950, as the Korean conflict heated into the Korean War, Japan's economy improved. US contracts for shoes, clothes, machine parts, and weapons to support US soldiers in the war poured into Japan. A job opened up at a small bank in Nagasaki. Father got the job.

Mother had an idea to help the family too. She would bake buns, fill them with bean jam, and sell them at the market. Sachiko's morning job was to help Mother deliver the buns to the market before running off to school. After school, Sachiko had another job.

In the late afternoon, Sachiko patiently waited across the road from the Sakamoto Cemetery, the same cemetery where she and her family had huddled on that August day after the atomic bomb exploded. The Sanno Shrine was not far from sight, nor was the One-Legged Torii Gate and the ancient camphor trees.

By ones and twos, children trudged up the hilly road toward Sachiko and the cemetery. Some were as young as seven, others as old as ten. All were skinny and filthy in their tattered clothes. All were war orphans who lived on the streets alone or in gangs, shining shoes, picking up cigarette butts to resell, or stealing whatever they could. They had no homes, no one to care for them, and no one to send them off to school.

Many Nagasaki families built shacks from the wreckage left on the spot where their house had once stood. This photo was taken on September 14, 1945.

Teacher Sachiko gathered her small group of students around her as they sat in the dirt. From her collection, Sachiko handed each orphan a discarded nail she had found on the ground.

"Again," Sachiko would say as the orphans dug their nails into the soft dirt. They practiced writing their names. Adding sums. Subtracting numbers.

"Again," Sachiko would say, remembering how Mother had taught her.

The children rubbed out their work and tried harder.

One day Sachiko asked the war orphans, "Where were you when the bomb dropped?" The children stared at her with empty eyes. They had forgotten. All they could remember were the people they had lost: their brothers, sisters, mothers, and fathers.

What would have happened to her if she had lost Mother and Father?

Sachiko didn't need to ask. She knew the answer.

What could she teach these children that Mother and Father had taught her? What words of her parents would Sachiko never forget? Sachiko gathered the orphans around her and began:

> *This is the only world we can live in.*
> *Hate only produces hate.*
> *No matter what the circumstances—good or bad—keep your own mind.*

Never let anyone scratch your mind.
Study.
Learn.
Pay attention to your teachers.
Your teachers will guide you.

The orphans were not the only children on Sachiko's mind. She worried about her younger sister. Nine-year-old Misa still wasn't well enough to go to school. She'd been too ill to ever attend.

Five years had passed since the atomic bomb blast, but many adults and children still suffered. Articles about the atomic bomb's effects on health were censored. But censorship could not erase the continued symptoms of radiation exposure: fatigue, dizziness, headaches, numbness, insomnia—and cancer.

Misa had cancer of the blood—leukemia.

What could Mother and Father do for their daughter? With no money to

Many children were left homeless and orphaned after the atomic bombings. Estimates of the number of orphans in Hiroshima range from four thousand to five thousand. Records for Nagasaki are sparse. This Hiroshima photo is from September 1945.

spare for medical care and nowhere to go for help, Father and Mother worried. So did Sachiko. She knew how to help the orphans, but what could she do to make her own sister happy? After teaching the orphan children, Sachiko would teach Misa all the songs she learned at school. Misa had told Sachiko that singing made her feel alive. As they sang together, Sachiko wondered what else she could do for Misa.

Sachiko with her sixth-grade teacher

Four years passed, and Misa grew deathly ill. Sachiko was frantic to do something. If she could grant Misa one wish, what would it be? Sachiko had an idea. She spoke to her high school music teacher.

The day the next music class was scheduled, fifteen-year-old Sachiko squatted beside Misa's futon. Misa reached up, wrapped her arms around Sachiko's neck, and climbed onto her back. Misa was finally going to school.

When Sachiko arrived at the classroom, Misa was too weak to sit up. As she slid off Sachiko's back, classmates rushed to push chairs together so Misa could lie down.

The music lesson began. Everyone sang, including Misa, in a soft, weak voice.

Misa's wish had come true.

But the lesson proved too taxing for Misa. Sachiko carried her sister home, sat beside her futon, washed her face, and held her hand.

Misa slowly turned her head toward Sachiko. "Thank you," Misa whispered, her last words.

By the end of her special day at school, Misa—Sachiko's little sister, her *imoto*, was dead.

Toshi. Aki. Ichiro. Uncle. Now Misa. Sachiko felt numb, as if trapped like a cicada in a net of death.

Misa. Gone.

Sachiko tried to cry, but she was empty of tears.

THE COLD WAR, KOREA, AND THE BOMB

After the Hiroshima and Nagasaki bombings, many people around the globe began to worry about the future. What would a world that now included nuclear weapons look like? Physicist J. Robert Oppenheimer, head of the Los Alamos laboratory in New Mexico where the atomic bombs had been developed, urged Truman to create international controls on nuclear weapons. Physicist Albert Einstein advised Truman to share scientific knowledge broadly to avoid a nuclear arms race.

In August 1946, the *New Yorker* magazine published an article by investigative journalist John Hersey. Called "Hiroshima," the article described the experiences of six Hiroshima survivors. For the first time, Americans had an up-close view of what it meant to live through nuclear war. Hersey's article was then republished as a book. Within six months, one million copies had sold. The American public began to question the moral implications of the atomic bombings.

To quell the growing concerns, the Truman administration published an article in *Harper's Magazine*, written by Secretary of War Henry Stimson, defending the decision to drop the bomb. The article claimed that

1. the devastation of the atomic bombs was the primary reason for Japan's surrender;
2. the bombings had made the sea and land invasion of Japan unnecessary, saving thousands, perhaps even one million American lives; and
3. the atomic bomb was the only weapon that would shock Japan into immediate surrender, so the US government felt it had no other military option.

With limited information to the contrary, the American public accepted the explanation. It became the accepted American narrative to describe the end of World War II in the Pacific.

Meanwhile, a new kind of world war was brewing—the Cold War. The United States and the Soviet Union had emerged from World War II as the world's two major superpowers. Former allies, the two nations became bitter enemies. The capitalist democracy of the United States supported Western Europe. The Communist Soviet Union, on the other hand, dominated Eastern European countries. An "iron curtain" of distrust fell, dividing Europe into East and West. The two worlds, closed off from each other, competed for military, economic, political, and cultural dominance. The competition over building strong militaries was known as the arms race.

The Cold War also divided Asia. After World War II, Korea was separated along the 38th parallel into two nations. The Soviet Union supported North Korea, while the United States backed South Korea. In 1950 North Korean troops invaded South Korea. The Korean War, the first military action of the Cold War, had begun. The Soviet Union provided support to North Korean troops. The United States sent troops to South Korea, and US B-29 bombers capable of carrying nuclear weapons flew over the Pacific. But would the United States use the bomb in this new war?

At a press conference on November 30, 1950, President Truman faced this question. He knew that the Soviets had developed and tested an atomic bomb the year before.

Mindful of the possibilities of a wider war with the Soviet Union or even a World War III, Truman answered the reporter's question carefully. "I don't want to see it used. It is a terrible weapon and it should not be used on innocent men, women, and children who have nothing whatever to do with this military aggression. That happens when it is used."

In July 1953, the Korean War ended in an uneasy armistice, with no clear winner. The country remained divided at the 38th parallel between north and south. Nuclear war had been averted.

The Korean War began only five years after the end of World War II. Here US bombers attack North Korean warehouses in about 1951.

FATHER

In 1955, the tenth anniversary of the atomic bombings of Hiroshima and Nagasaki, an enormous bronze statue was unveiled in Nagasaki's new Peace Park, close to the hypocenter of the bombing. The statue was of a man whose left hand stretched out horizontally, representing hope for an elusive, eternal peace. His right hand pointed to the sky, warning of the danger of nuclear weapons and the arms race.

Every day Sachiko looked up in the sky and remembered Aki, Ichiro, Misa, Toshi, and Uncle.

"There is no life in the world we can waste." Father told Sachiko. "Use your wonderful life to help people in the world. Every life is precious."

"Face forward. Keep walking. Then you will see the light of hope," Father urged her.

Sachiko did her best. She turned her back on her tragic memories, faced forward, graduated from high school, and accepted a job with a good salary as an accountant at a large Nagasaki company. Father still had his job at the bank. Now Sachiko had a job. The future did look brighter facing forward.

At the age of eighteen, Sachiko didn't talk about the past. She thought that by not talking about what had happened, she wouldn't have to remember the agony she experienced. Sachiko walked past new buildings and crossed newly paved streets, wearing high heels, a stylish skirt and blouse, and a hat with a saucy tilt. No one would have guessed Sachiko had been a six-year-old girl buried and choking under rubble. No one would have guessed she was a *hibakusha.*

The Peace Statue at the Nagasaki Peace Park was created by sculptor Seibou Kitamura, a Nagasaki native. Each year a memorial service is conducted in front of the statue.

People who had survived the atomic explosions of Hiroshima and Nagasaki were called hibakusha, literally translated as "explosion-affected people." Survivors were hibakusha if they 1) had survived the bomb blast itself; 2) had lived 2 to 3 miles (3.2 to 4.8 km) away from the explosion and were exposed to radiation; 3) had entered Hiroshima or Nagasaki within two weeks of the bomb's explosion, which exposed them to radiation; or 4) were born just after the atomic bomb to mothers who had survived. Father, Mother, Sachiko, and other hibakusha would live with the effects of the atomic bomb for the rest of their lives.

Hibakusha with the thick keloids left by thermal burns hid their scars under long-sleeved shirts and sweaters. Those with shiny scalps, on which hair would never grow again, wore hats in public.

Young men worried about marrying and starting families with hibakusha women. Young women worried about marrying and starting families with hibakusha men. They remembered the stunted morning glories that had grown the summer after the bomb. They wondered, Would their babies be affected by the bomb too?

No one wanted to talk about what worried them most, the effect of the radiation inside them.

Father had been silent too.

He didn't want to talk about how fatigue had sapped his energy. But Mother had noticed. Father had lost weight. His skin had turned yellow. He'd grown nauseous and feverish.

"Go to the public baths and soak," Mother urged. "You'll feel better."

But Father was too tired to go to the baths.

"Then lie down on the tatami mat and rest," Mother suggested. She cooled Father with her fan.

Father thought resting in the shade of the camphor boughs would be more pleasant, but he did not have the energy to go to the camphors. He was too ill to do anything but collapse.

Sachiko and Mother rushed him to the hospital. The doctor examined him.

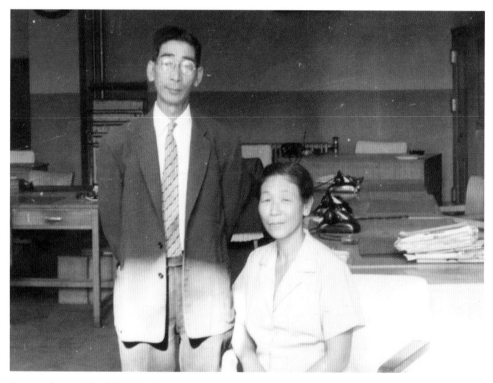

A rare photo of Sachiko's father and mother taken around 1950

Liver cancer. The effect of the bomb's radiation was still inside of him.

"No, not Father," Sachiko whispered. What would she do without him? His death would be like losing her two arms. How would she go on?

Father's cancer was advanced, and he soon fell into a coma. Day after day, Mother and Sachiko sat next to Father's hospital bed, hoping, praying, and holding each other as Father lay still in his bed.

Twelve days later, on September 11, 1961, without another word to Sachiko to point the way, Father—Sachiko's *otosan*—died.

Mother turned to Sachiko. "Now you must be like Father."

SACHIKO

1961–1962

Be like Father?

Sachiko's heart felt heavy and empty. How could she be like Father? She could only miss him.

Even the towering camphor trees could not offer Sachiko strength to face forward. In her early twenties, Sachiko felt depleted and tired, as if she were moving in slow motion. But didn't everyone in Nagasaki feel exhausted?

On Mother's urging, Sachiko visited a doctor. He felt her neck and glands, and frowned. He removed a small sample of her thyroid cells and took the cells to the laboratory for evaluation.

Sachiko waited for a diagnosis. She was stunned by the results.

Thyroid cancer.

How was this possible? She had no pain, no great swelling in her neck, no warning of illness—just terrible, terrible fatigue.

The effect of the bomb's radiation was still inside her.

In Hiroshima and Nagasaki, doctors counted and graphed the number of hibakusha with thyroid and other cancers. They suspected that these cancers were related to radiation exposure, and they observed that the rate of thyroid cancer was increasing in these two cities.

Sachiko's diagnosis was not a matter of scientific study. She needed immediate treatment. The tumor in her thyroid gland had to be removed quickly, before the disease spread.

Sachiko at about twenty-one years old

Sachiko had surgery. While she lay on the operating table in the hospital, Mother knelt at a nearby shrine. She pressed her hands together and prayed.

Sachiko opened her eyes in the hospital recovery room. Searing pain gripped her throat. Fear tangled her mind. On her bed, she could hardly breathe. Barely swallow. It was as if she were under the pile of rubble after the atomic bomb had exploded. Sachiko opened her mouth to call for help, but no words came.

None.

Memories flashed of that hot summer day on August 9, 1945, playing house and making mud dumplings with her friends.

The explosion.

Heat.

Wind pressing her down.

Stones, glass, leaves, branches, roof tiles piling on top of her.

The screams.

The burning.

The dark silence of the Sakamoto Cemetery. Shivering, huddling next to Mother. Sachiko had not said a word then, either.

Lying on her hospital bed, Sachiko opened her mouth again to speak, but no sound came. Despair spread over her like thick dust.

A nurse arrived and offered a notepad and pen. What would Sachiko like to write?

This is not the life I want.

Weeks passed in the hospital. Each day Mother brought miso soup. Each day doctors and nurses came to examine Sachiko. During one visit, Sachiko managed a breathy grunt. "You're going to be all right," the doctor assured her.

Would she?

Sachiko still could not speak. In her mind, she wandered in a dark world, alone, afraid of the future.

Who am I without a voice? Sachiko wondered.

One month later, Sachiko left the hospital and returned home with Mother. Everything looked familiar. The small cooking stove. Grandmother's green leaf bowl. The boxes of her brothers' ashes. Uncle's. Misa's. Father's. But without her voice, Sachiko felt lost—alone.

At night, her mind filled with dark thoughts. How could she ever face forward again? How could she resume her life? Take care of Mother? Go back to work? In the middle of the night, Sachiko shrank smaller and smaller, sank deeper and deeper into the darkness. The door to possibilities seemed shut tight.

In the middle of one of those nights, something shifted in Sachiko's mind. A familiar voice whispered a forgotten message: "Listen to your teachers. They will guide you."

Father's words.

In spirit, Father was still with her, but who could her teachers be now?

ALL THE WORLD IS SUFFERING.
IT IS ALSO FULL OF THE OVERCOMING.
—HELEN KELLER

A clouded image formed in Sachiko's memory and grew clearer. A beautiful woman with round eyes, a brilliant smile, and a hat tilting on her head—Helen Keller stood tall at the Nagasaki Train Station.

Deaf, blind Helen Keller knew nothing but darkness and silence, yet she had stood with outstretched arms, smiling, offering hope to thousands, and speaking with her own voice. Helen Keller once wrote, "When one door of happiness closes, another opens; but often we look so long at the closed door that we do not see the one which has been opened for us." Helen Keller had found her voice.

Could Sachiko find hers?

Sachiko began her "everyday training," as she called it. Swallowing was excruciating, but every day, she practiced trying to speak, moving beyond grunts to whispers. On her own, she experimented with pitch, sound, and volume. Sachiko imagined climbing a mountain. Where was she along the path forward and up? How long would it take to climb to the top? Two months? Four? Sachiko matched her own determination with Helen's, cultivating optimism and hope. After six months of training, Sachiko's vocal cords had strengthened enough to speak words. After that came sentences. Finally, she could talk again.

Sachiko learned what Helen Keller had already known. Every word is precious.

LONG-TERM EFFECTS OF RADIATION

No one knew the full effects of radiation exposure on the human body after an atomic blast. Broken bones mend. Severe cuts and burns can eventually heal, but exposure to full-body radiation affects the body for a lifetime. Radioactive waves penetrate the skin, moving into the bones and bloodstream and into the body's cells. Inside the nucleus of a cell is deoxyribonucleic acid (DNA), which is a cell's carrier of genetic information. Radiation damages DNA. Cells may then reproduce abnormally, later leading to cancer and other diseases.

After the atomic bombings in Japan, children who had been exposed to the radiation were particularly vulnerable to certain cancers. For example, hibakusha who had been three-fourths of a mile (1.2 km) from the hypocenter had a 40 to 50 percent chance of developing one of several types of cancer. A child survivor younger than ten years old who was 1 mile (1.6 km) from the hypocenter had an 18 percent higher risk of a leukemia diagnosis than did people who had not been exposed to the radiation. Doctors also noted a marked increase in rates of thyroid cancer, specifically in those who were children at the time of the blast.

In 1946 President Truman ordered the establishment of the Atomic Bomb Casualty Commission (ABCC). The goal of the commission was for American doctors to go to Japan to observe and track the lifelong effects of radiation on atomic bomb survivors. Along with Japanese physicians, the American doctors examined survivors, asked questions about their atomic bomb experiences, calculated the distance they were from the hypocenter, and charted medical observations.

Over the years, ABCC doctors documented the thick, itchy, and painful keloids that had healed over the thermal burns of the hibakusha. They observed cataracts

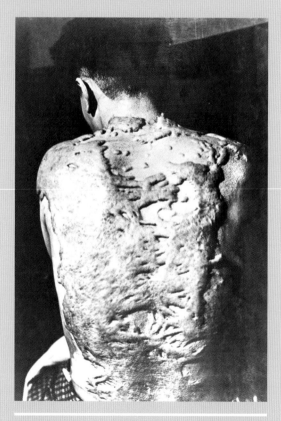

Keloids cover the back of a survivor of the Nagasaki atomic bomb. Keloids are dense, fibrous growths that grow over scar tissue.

in damaged eyes and noted birth defects in the children born in the months after the bombing. And they diagnosed cancers: skin cancer, lung cancer, stomach cancer, breast cancer, liver cancer, thyroid cancer, and leukemia.

Under ABCC rules, American physicians were not permitted to share their growing database of clinical knowledge with Japanese physicians nor were ABCC doctors allowed to treat their patients' illnesses. They were there simply to collect information. Hibakusha felt deep distrust of American ABCC doctors. With no offers of medical treatment, many hibakusha felt the ABCC had reduced them to numbers on a chart rather than people in need of help.

Doctors wondered how long it would take to fully understand the long-term effects of radiation on the human body. Dr. James Yamazaki, the third director of Nagasaki's ABCC program and a Japanese American citizen, summarized the situation: "We must wait . . . until the end of the normal life span of the youngest survivor before we can know the full story of the effects on those exposed to the radiation of the bomb. . . . No one can say how much longer it might take for defects to show up in succeeding generations."

James Yamazaki spent his long medical career studying the impact of nuclear explosions and radiation on children. After his work in Nagasaki, Yamazaki studied the effects of radiation from nuclear testing on children of the Marshall Islands. He has become an antiwar activist and an advocate for the elimination of nuclear weapons.

A PATH TO PEACE

1962

Sachiko was a survivor. She had conquered thyroid cancer. She had her voice back. She could speak. She was ready to live again, but an important question nagged, unanswered. Now that she could speak, what would she use her voice for?

"This is the only world we can live in. Never say evil words, otherwise we'll not see peace. Hate only produces hate." Father's words echoed again.

Sachiko heard Father's voice all around her. Under the camphor trees. On her study rock. In the garden carved out of rubble.

Sachiko pondered Father's words—the only treasures he could offer her. She dug through her memories. What else had he told her?

"You are too young to read Gandhi's works, but one day you must study Gandhi. You will learn something you will need the rest of your life."

Sachiko remembered the moment Father had said those words, in February 1948. Sachiko was nine. The two of them had stood in the garden of rubble. Father's eyes were full of sorrow as he placed his strong hand on her shoulder and told her Gandhi had died.

Sachiko remembered reading Gandhi for herself for the first time at the edge of the Sakamoto Cemetery. Orange streaks from the bomb's intense heat still marred the cemetery's stone wall. Sitting in the quiet of replanted trees. Memories of war were everywhere. Sachiko opened her Gandhi book. She read, "The only weapon that can save the world is nonviolence."

A photograph of Gandhi as a little boy with ears sticking out offered no clues to the great man he would become. The boy sat stiffly in a chair and

Nagasaki's Sakamoto International Cemetery, where Sachiko often studied

stared at the camera with dark, intense eyes. By his own admission, Gandhi had been timid and afraid of the dark as a boy. At night, he slept with a light on. Gandhi wrote, "I used to be very shy and avoid all company. My books and my lessons were my sole companions. To be at school at the stroke of the hour and run back as soon as school closed—that was my daily habit. I literally ran back, because I could not bear to talk to anybody. I was even afraid lest anyone should poke fun at me."

Hadn't Sachiko felt the same when she was a child? Already, she felt close to Gandhi.

She read on.

Having studied law in England, Gandhi returned to India. During his very first legal case, he rose before the judge to defend his client. His nerves jangled so much he was struck speechless, and not a word came out of his mouth.

Speechless?

Sachiko felt an instant connection. Gandhi had struggled too.

Sachiko continued reading.

In 1893, at the age of twenty-three, Gandhi left India to seek work in South Africa. The day Gandhi arrived, he boarded a train to the capital city of Pretoria. Wearing clothes of an Englishman, Gandhi sat in a first-class car, holding a first-class ticket. A white man boarded the same car, took one look at Gandhi, and demanded the conductor send the "dirty coolie" back to third class. Gandhi refused to move. The conductor picked him up and threw him off the train.

During the bitterly cold night that followed, Gandhi sat on a bench, playing the humiliating incident over and over in his mind. As dawn approached, an idea tempered Gandhi's anger. He began to understand prejudice and discrimination in a way he had not understood them before. Yes, Gandhi had been a victim of hate when the men threw him off the train. But the men were tainted too—by their own hatred. Everyone's life was made small and ugly by prejudice and discrimination, whether the person realized it or not.

Gandhi at the age of seven

Gandhi's ideas shifted. Fighting discrimination was what was important, not fighting the men on the train. But how does one small person fight something as big as prejudice?

Gandhi pondered these ideas some more. By the time morning arrived, he had made up his mind. Never again would he endure discrimination against himself—or anyone else. He would fight back—not with violence but with a deep, bottomless love for the human race and the unshakable truth that hate and discrimination must be overcome.

Gandhi had found his voice.

Reading Gandhi, Sachiko's heart opened to a new way of thinking, a way of being in the world. Despite the pain she had suffered from war, the

With radioactive exposure from drifting nuclear fallout, all Japanese felt threatened. Anger rippled through the country, and citizens began drafting petitions against nuclear testing. For the first time since 1945, a small group of hibakusha from Hiroshima and Nagasaki publicly told their stories and pleaded for the abolition of nuclear weapons. The demand for "never again" grew louder.

By 1957 Britain had tested its first atomic and hydrogen bombs. Three years later, France tested its first atomic bomb. By 1960 the Soviet Union had a nuclear arsenal of 1,605 weapons. The United States' arsenal held 18,638 nuclear warheads.

Antinuclear marches and rallies spread through Europe and the United States. In 1957 nearly one hundred thousand people in Britain protested against the hydrogen bomb. In 1961 fifty thousand women marched against nuclear weapons in sixty different US cities. More protests would follow. The nuclear arms race escalated as China, India, Pakistan, and North Korea eventually developed their own nuclear weapons too.

How much longer would nations pave the way for the mutually assured destruction of nuclear warfare? And what could any one person do for peace?

Antinuclear protesters near Times Square in New York City on February 1, 1962

CICADA YEARS

1968–1992

Cicada nymphs live many years underground. Protected under the earth, the young cicadas sip nutrients from the tips of tree roots. In time, they tunnel their way up through the layers of earth to the branches of trees. In the light of the sun, the cicadas step out of their thin shells, dry their wings, and sing their summer song.

Sachiko remained silent about her experience surviving the atomic bomb, her suffering. Like a cicada nymph, Sachiko sipped the nutrients from the roots of Father's wisdom; Helen Keller's courage; and Gandhi and Martin Luther King Jr.'s beliefs in love, nonviolence, and justice.

A decade slipped by.

Sachiko faced forward and applied for a job as an accountant at the well-respected Maruzen Bookstore. The store was known for its wide-ranging intellectual and academic books from the West. She got the job. In her office, Sachiko worked quickly and efficiently at the bookstore's accounts, adding sums and compiling book orders. The radio played in the background. On her lunch breaks, Sachiko listened to the news on the radio and browsed the bookstore shelves. Which authors might help her see the world in a new light? Which books should she buy for further study? The more she read, the more her ideas deepened.

During this time, Sachiko rose early in the morning to read the newspaper and take care of Mother. Each August 9, Sachiko and Mother filled Grandmother's bowl with ice. Each August 9, a quiet unease filled Sachiko. What should she do with her memories of the bomb? What real purpose could they serve?

Other hibakusha were asking the same questions. A few hibakusha leaders stepped forward to share their experiences of survival, and they encouraged others to do the same.

As ice and memories melted in Grandmother's bowl, the phone would ring with requests. Would Sachiko share her hibakusha experience? Would she talk with schoolchildren? The children need to know her story.

Sachiko would answer no—not yet. No, she would not want to say anything that might bring dishonor to Father or Mother. No, Mother needed her. Mother was ill, diagnosed with leukemia.

Yet silence ate at Sachiko as the urge to tell her story grew.

The view over the Nagasaki harbor in 1960. As Nagasaki rebuilt, signs of atomic destruction faded, but memories remained vivid for those who had experienced the blast.

Sachiko faithfully read the newspaper and listened to news on the radio. In 1989 Emperor Hirohito died. All of Japan witnessed an end to an era. In 1991 the Soviet Union and its Communist empire collapsed. The Cold War was over. A long chapter in history had ended. A new one would begin.

What would war mean now for the world? And peace?

No one could predict the future, but Sachiko knew this: the world must never again see nuclear war.

Never.

But how could the world get to "never again?" And what could Sachiko do that would make a difference?

Sachiko pondered these questions.

Then, in 1992, Mother, Sachiko's *okasan*, died.

With Mother's death, Sachiko became her family's only witness to tell their story. The responsibility was heavy. With all that dwelled in Sachiko's heart, if she had another chance to speak, what would she say?

Sachiko sat alone in her house without Mother. Memories flashed. The egg. Little Toshi clapping his hands. Playing house. The bomb blast. Toshi. Ichiro. Aki. Uncle. Misa. Father. Mother.

Ichiro's last words: "Take care of everyone."

But how?

Sachiko had needed years to crawl out of the dark into the light and find her voice. She envisioned

One of the most recognizable sounds of summer in Japan is the buzzing song of the cicada.

her personal teachers of peace—Father, Helen Keller, Mohandas Gandhi, and Martin Luther King Jr. What would they have advised?

YOU MUST BE THE CHANGE
YOU WISH TO SEE IN THE WORLD.
—GANDHI

THE FIFTIETH ANNIVERSARY

The year 1995 marked the fiftieth anniversary of the atomic bombings of Hiroshima and Nagasaki and the end of World War II. Japanese and Americans alike faced the anniversary with lingering memories of the tragic events of the war and unresolved emotions.

To prepare for the fiftieth anniversary, citizens throughout Japan organized peace demonstrations. They proposed conferences calling for the abolition of nuclear weapons. In Nagasaki, emotions ran high. Six years earlier, Nagasaki's popular, outspoken mayor, Hitoshi Motoshima, had criticized Emperor Hirohito for his responsibility in bringing on the war. In 1990 Motoshima was shot and wounded by an angry citizen demanding that Japan militarily rearm.

Controversy surged again as Japan prepared for the Nagasaki Atomic Bomb Museum, which was to open in 1996. Some Japanese critics felt that the exhibition focused too narrowly on the hibakusha experience of the war. In response, the museum planned to add previously undisclosed research about Japanese soldiers' wartime brutality in Asia. Among the topics to explore, the museum would document the Nanjing Massacre and the Allied POWs forced Bataan Death March. The museum's proposal caused a furor among many politically conservative Japanese.

The Nagasaki Atomic Bomb Museum

Since August 9, 1995, Sachiko Yasui has traveled throughout Japan, to Canada, and to the United States, sharing her experience with thousands of students; lecturing at universities; and giving newspaper, radio, and television interviews. In 2005, the sixtieth anniversary of the dropping of the bombs, Sachiko became president of the Keisho-bu Branch of the Nagasaki Foundation for the Promotion of Peace, an organization that supports the public sharing of hibakusha experiences. She served as president of the organization until 2013, telling her story and working to promote peace.

In 2014 Sachiko offered this advice to the young people of the world:

WHAT IS PEACE?
WHAT KIND OF PERSON SHOULD I BE?
KEEP PURSUING ANSWERS TO THESE QUESTIONS.

AUTHOR'S NOTE

I am often asked how I met Sachiko Yasui and came to write her story. The simple answer is that I met Sachiko in Minneapolis in 2005. Five years later, I wrote her a letter and proposed we work together on a book about her experience—and she agreed.

The more complex answer is this:

I've had a personal relationship with World War II since I was a little girl. I knew of distant Jewish relatives in Poland who most likely died in Nazi concentration camps. As a young captain in the American infantry, my father had fought as a rifleman throughout Nazi Germany. My father never shared his war stories with me, but in the middle of the night, I heard his nightmare screams through my bedroom wall.

In 2010 I met Dr. Takayuki Miyanishi, the Nagasaki president of the Saint Paul-Nagasaki Sister City Committee, at a potluck dinner in Saint Paul, Minnesota. Dr. Miyanishi agreed to help me connect with Sachiko, and if Sachiko agreed to our writing project, he would also be my interpreter when I visited Nagasaki.

In November 2010, I made my first trip to the city. Jet-lagged and nervous, I wasn't sure I would even recognize Sachiko. Sachiko greeted me at the city library, her eyes bright. She recognized me right away. Dr. Miyanishi joined us. My husband, Kim, was with us too. Our Sachiko team moved into a quiet room in the library to begin our journey together.

As is the custom of Japan, Sachiko and I exchanged gifts. I brought matching necklaces as a sign of friendship. Sachiko gave me a *kokeshi* doll. Carved from a solid piece of wood, painted a shiny black, the round wooden doll fit in the palm of my hand. Her little black dots for eyes peered up at me. The doll became our talisman, our symbolic universal child, ready to hear Sachiko's story. I placed the doll in the middle of the table amid the recording equipment. Each time I visited Sachiko,

Sachiko Yasui and Caren Stelson at their first meeting in Nagasaki in 2010

114

I would bring the kokeshi back to Nagasaki. The first time I brought the doll back, Sachiko clapped her hands. Later, she said, "I knew I could tell you everything."

"Tell me what Nagasaki was like when you were little," I asked during that first meeting. I opened my notebook to write. Sachiko began with the egg. The hen had finally laid an egg. Little brother Toshi clapped his hands.

I traveled to Nagasaki five times to visit Sachiko, once each year, beginning with my first trip in 2010. The first four trips followed a similar pattern. For two full days, sometimes three, Sachiko; Dr. Miyanishi; my husband, Kim; and I would gather around a table with recording equipment. We would begin wherever we had left off, asking questions, digging deeper, going beyond the details of Sachiko's usual public lectures. Dr. Miyanishi would simultaneously translate as Sachiko spoke. When I asked to see Grandmother's bowl, Sachiko brought the bowl the next day to our recording session. She told me it was the first time she had shown the bowl to anyone. When we talked about little sister Misa and her death, Sachiko cried. It was the first time, Sachiko said, that she had cried for her sister. It had taken nearly sixty years for tears.

As Dr. Miyanishi translated Sachiko's story, his words had a musical cadence, a hint of haiku poetry, and references to nature. The cicadas made their appearances in Sachiko's story as they did when we visited the Nagasaki Peace Park and the Nagasaki Atomic Bomb Museum. The sounds of cicadas followed us as we toured Sachiko's neighborhood, strolled through the Sakamoto International Cemetery, and visited the One-Legged Torii, the Sanno Shrine, and the camphor trees. Today the city of Nagasaki celebrates the camphor trees as natural monuments, having inspired survivors of the atomic bomb to rebuild their lives. At night, as I watched streetlights flicker like fireflies along Nagasaki's modern harbor, I reflected upon the remarkable resiliency of the human spirit.

My study of Sachiko's story and World War II in the Pacific led me beyond Nagasaki. In 2012 I received a scholarship to travel to Hiroshima to participate in the Hiroshima City University's weeklong peace symposium. With thousands from all over the world, I would also attend the August 6 commemoration at the Hiroshima Peace Memorial Park. In New York City, I visited the American Foundation for the Blind and the Helen Keller Archives. In Hawaii I visited Pearl Harbor and toured the USS *Missouri,* the battleship on which the surrender of the Empire of Japan took place.

Telling Sachiko's story prompted me to think more broadly about war and peace. With the help of Keiko Kawakami, my Minneapolis translator and a University of

Minnesota Japanese language instructor, I read the lectures Sachiko had delivered at Nagasaki University. I also read articles about her. I read the writings of Helen Keller and poured over the works of Gandhi and Martin Luther King Jr. I spent hours reading about World War II in the Pacific, unlearning and relearning history. Wartime censorship and propaganda have skewed our understanding of why the United States chose to drop the atomic bombs. As American historian John Dower writes, "No one denies that these policy makers desired to hasten the war's end and to save American lives, but no serious historian regards those as the sole considerations driving the use of the bombs on Japanese cities."

While Sachiko's story began more than sixty years ago, it remains extremely relevant. According to the Ploughshares Fund, a global organization working to prevent the spread and use of nuclear weapons, nine countries in 2016 hold a total of 15,695 nuclear weapons in their military stockpiles. The United States and Russia hold 94 percent of these weapons.

In the late fall of 2013, I received a startling e-mail. Sachiko had had a stroke. By early January 2014, I was on my fifth trip to Nagasaki. Keiko Kawakami, the kokeshi doll, and I sat together in a Nagasaki hospital room with Sachiko. Nurses scurried about. Raised up on pillows, Sachiko spoke of Helen Keller, Gandhi, and Martin Luther King Jr. The nurses were amazed.

During that visit, I met a woman named Etsuko Matsuo, Sachiko's youngest sister. I also met Etsuko's young granddaughter Kanon. I had no idea Sachiko had a surviving sister. Etsuko had been born after the war and had not experienced the horrors of the atomic bombing of August 9, 1945. Sachiko and Etsuko had a pact that Sachiko's story would focus only on the family members who had experienced the atomic bomb. Etsuko helped me to stay in touch with Sachiko as she continued her recovery and moved to a nursing home. Memory has shaped Sachiko's story. Etsuko's memories too are treasures.

Sachiko's story has come to an end, but not my Sachiko journey. I've made many friends in Nagasaki, especially Sachiko, who will always call me back to Japan. I have too long a reading list to stop studying war and peace. Sachiko's story and our friendship have changed me irrevocably. In the end, I have found my own pathways to peace. Perhaps this was the gift I was looking for all along.

FAMILY TREE

GLOSSARY OF JAPANESE WORDS

Japanese words in this book are written using the Hepburn romanization system. Japanese writing is a combination of three character types: hiragana, katakana, and kanji. The Japanese spellings of words in the glossary below are primarily written with hiragana characters. The words *chokoreto* and *pikadon* are written with katakana characters. Kanon's name in the dedication is written in kanji.

Note: "ooh" represents an "o" sound held longer than "oh"

arigato ありがとう: (ah-ree-gah-toh) thank you

chokoreto チョコレート: (cho-koh-reh-toh) chocolate

genshi bakudan げんしばくだん: (gehn-shee ba-koo-dahn) atomic bomb

hibakusha ひばくしゃ: (hee-bah-koo-shah) explosion-affected people; a term for those who survived the bombings of Hiroshima and Nagasaki

imoto いもうと: (ee-mooh-toh) little sister

kamikaze かみかぜ: (kah-mee-kah-zay) Japanese pilots who were assigned to crash their planes into targets during World War II

kokeshi こけし: (koh-kay-shee) traditional Japanese wooden dolls

kudasai ください: (koo-dah-sigh) please give me

mizu みず: (mee-zoo) water

monpe もんぺ: (mohn-pay) a style of pants

moshi moshi もしもし: (moh-shee moh-shee) hello (when answering the phone)

nisei にせい: (nee-say) a son or daughter of Japanese immigrants who is born and educated in the United States or other countries in North America or South America

ohayo おはよう: (oh-hi-yooh) good morning

ojisan おじさん: (oh-jee-sahn) uncle

okasan おかあさん: (oh-kah-sahn) mother

onisan おにいさん: (oh-nee-sahn) older brother

otosan おとうさん: (oh-toh-sahn) father

ototo おとうと: (oh-tooh-toh) younger brother

pikadon ピカドン: (pee-kah-don) a word that refers specifically to the explosion of an atomic bomb; *pika* means "brilliant light" and *don* means "boom"

sayonara さよなら: (sigh-yo-nah-rah) good-bye

Shinto しんとう: (shin-tooh) the traditional religion of Japan

tasukete kudasai たすけてください: (tah-su-keh-tay koo-dah-sigh) please help me

tatami たたみ: (tah-tah-mee) a straw mat used as a floor covering

tekki てっき: (teh-kee) enemy plane

tempura てんぷら: (tem-puh-ruh) food coated in batter and deep fried

tonarigumi となりぐみ: (toh-nah-ree-goo-mee) neighborhood association

torii とりい: (toh-ree) a gate at the entrance to a Shinto shrine

tsunami つなみ: (tsu-nah-mee) a high, large ocean wave that can cause immense destruction when it reaches land

udon うどん: (oo-don) a thick noodle made from wheat flour

umi yukaba うみゆかば: (oo-mee yoo-kah-bah) "if I go to the sea," the first line of a patriotic Japanese song that was popular during World War II

Yamato やまと: (yah-mah-toh) a term historically used within Japan to refer to the country of Japan; in the late 1800s, it was used to refer to a race of people who lived on the home islands of Japan

NOTES

The main narrative of this book is based on my interviews with Sachiko Yasui in Nagasaki, which took place over the course of five visits between July 2010 and January 2014, as well as additional communication with her via letters and phone calls through April 2016. Sachiko has read through the narrative chapters (translated into Japanese) and confirmed their accuracy. Unless otherwise stated, the information in the chapters about Sachiko's life comes from our interviews and correspondence.

Additionally, I've cited my sources for historical information that may not be widely known. Full publication information for all books listed here appears in the bibliography. Readers will also find additional information about historic events that parallel Sachiko's story. I hope these extra details will both clarify events and encourage readers to dig deeper into history on their own.

Throughout the book, Japanese names have been written in Western style, first name then family name. Nicknames of Sachiko's brothers and sister have been used rather than their given names because those are the names she used when she spoke of them.

HOME IN NAGASAKI

10: No one in Japan had enough to eat: Collingham, *The Taste of War*, 310; Southard, *Nagasaki: Life after Nuclear War*, 7.

10: "Umi Yukaba": The lyrics of "Umi Yukaba," are based on a classical Japanese poem that was set to music in 1937. During the Pacific War, "Umi Yukaba" became the anthem of Japan's Imperial Navy. It was sung to kamikaze pilots as they took off on their suicide missions. A *YouTube* search for "Umi Yukaba," will turn up several versions. The translation of "Umi Yukaba" was taken from "Umi Yukaba," *Wikipedia*, February 15, 2016, https://en.wikipedia.org/wiki/Umi_Yukaba.

WORLD WAR II

11: Name of the war: World War II's Pacific War was known by other names. The Allied forces also referred to the war as the Pacific Theater, the War in the Pacific, or the War against Japan. Japan often used the name Great East Asia War. Before 1941 the war in Asia is also often referred to as the Second Sino-Japanese War.

11: After wars with China (1894–1895) and Russia (1904–1905): After winning the Sino-Japanese War in 1895, Japan gained the island of Taiwan as a colony from China. After winning the Russo-Japanese War in 1905, Japan acquired part of the Manchuria Railway and adjacent land from Russia. In 1910 Japan officially annexed Korea, and in 1931, Manchuria (known at the time as Manchukuo) came under Japan's influence.

11: Emperor Hirohito: To better understand the role of Japan's emperor, the role of the military during the Pacific War, and issues of racism, readers will need to explore Japanese history.

The role of Japan's emperor evolved through the centuries. A transformational change came in 1868 when the Tokugawa shogun (great general) lost his power and the Meiji emperor was restored. (Meiji means "Enlightened Rule.") This began the period called the Meiji Restoration. The Meiji emperor was considered the head of Japan as well as the spiritual leader, although he did not rule directly. During this time, Japan replaced its feudal system with a highly centralized government and a powerful army and navy. Japan also modernized its social and economic institutions. As Japan grew stronger, it fought and won a war with China and Russia, becoming a colonial power over Korea and Taiwan. Western powers also saw opportunities for colonization in China and Southeast Asia and thwarted Japan's attempts to expand in Asia. Japan's anger toward the West paved a path of resentment and the willingness to gain power through military means.

When Hirohito took the throne in 1926, the Showa era began. (Showa means "Enlightened Peace.") During Hirohito's reign, the military gained greater power in the government, eventually ruling the country. By 1937 Japan had begun a full-scale war with China. Racism, anger, and a sense of superiority played a role in brutal warfare. During this time, the Imperial Japanese Army forced approximately two hundred thousand women, called comfort women into prostitution. Many of these women were Korean. Although Hirohito as the emperor remained the head of state throughout the Pacific War, it remains unclear how responsible he was for military decisions that doomed his country.

12: Torture and killing of millions of Chinese: During Japan's invasion of China in 1937, the Imperial Japanese Army brutally massacred and raped between forty thousand and three hundred thousand Chinese civilians in what is called the Rape of Nanjing or the Nanjing Massacre. (Nanjing is also sometimes spelled Nanking.) This attack began on December 13, 1937, and continued for seven weeks. Japanese records were kept secret or destroyed after the event, so historians have been unable to verify the exact number of people killed.

R. J. Rummel, professor of political science at the University of Hawaii, estimated that between 1937 and 1945, from three million to more than ten million people were killed by Japanese forces. For more information see "Statistics of Japanese Democide: Estimates, Calculations, and Sources," Statistics of Democide, https://www.hawaii.edu/powerkills /SOD.CHAP3.HTM.

13: Pearl Harbor attack: In December 1941, the European War and the Pacific War converged with Japan's attack on Pearl Harbor in Hawaii. Under Japan's Prime Minister Tojo, Admiral Isoroku Yamamoto became the primary architect in the planning of Pearl Harbor. As a young man, Yamamoto had attended Harvard University in Cambridge, Massachusetts. He spoke fluent English and had traveled throughout the United States studying American customs. Although Yamamoto's Pearl Harbor attack was a great success for the Japanese, the admiral had grave doubts about Japan going to war against the United States. He feared that America's military capability would eventually triumph over Japan.

The attack on the US Pacific Fleet at Pearl Harbor was not Japan's only military action against the West. In the weeks and months to follow, Japan launched attacks on Thailand; the US-held islands of the Philippines, Guam, and Wake Island; and the British colonies of Malaya, Singapore, Hong Kong, and Burma.

13: "A date which will live in infamy": "Teaching with Documents: A Date Which Will Live in Infamy," National Archives, https://www.archives.gov/education/lessons/day-of-infamy. (Interested readers can find the first typed draft of Roosevelt's speech as well as additional resources at this site.)

13: Allied powers: With war declared, the coalition of Allied nations was formalized in January 1942. The key Allied leaders were US president Franklin Delano Roosevelt, British prime minister Winston Churchill, and the Soviet premier Joseph Stalin. China's Generalissimo Chiang Kai-shek was also an important Allied player in the war with Japan.

The Axis powers of Germany, Italy, and Japan had a more loosely coordinated pact. In 1942 the leaders of the Axis countries were Germany's Fuhrer Adolph Hitler, Italy's Prime Minister Benito Mussolini, and Japan's Emperor Hirohito and Prime Minister Hideki Tojo. Although these leaders did not routinely meet, they agreed to recognize Germany's desire for dominance over Europe, Italy's dominance over the Mediterranean Sea, and Japan's over East Asia and the Pacific.

13: Soviet Union: From 1922 to 1991, the Soviet Union, officially known as the Union of Soviet Socialist Republics (USSR), was a union of multiple countries, which included Russia. During this time span, the Communist Party governed the Soviet Union. In 1991 the Soviet Union collapsed and separated into fifteen different countries, the largest of which is Russia.

13: No plans to stop until Japan surrendered: During the Pacific War, the United States led a long campaign of island battles advancing toward the home islands of Japan. One of the bitterest and bloodiest of the Pacific War was the Battle of Okinawa, which lasted eighty-two days (April 1–June 22, 1945). Approximately 12,000 Americans, 70,000 Japanese soldiers and Okinawan conscripts, and 100,000 to 150,000 Okinawan civilians were killed. The number of deaths on Okinawa was a warning. The stakes were high for both Japan and the United States should the United States invade Japan to win the war. For more information about the Battle of Okinawa and the experience of the Okinawans see "Civilians on Okinawa," *American Experience,* http://www.pbs.org/wgbh/americanexperience/features/general-article /pacific-civilians-okinawa.

RACISM AND WAR

14: Germany's genocide of six million European Jews: For more information, see the United States Holocaust Memorial Museum's website: https://www.ushmm.org/learn.

14: Anti-Japanese sentiment: For more information about perception of and treatment of Japanese Americans, see Reeves, *Infamy: The Shocking Story of the Japanese American Internment in World War II.*

14: Imprisonment of approximately 120,000 people of Japanese ancestry: Roosevelt called for the incarceration of Japanese Americans primarily living on the Pacific Coast of the United States. In Hawaii, where nearly 40 percent of the population was Japanese American, several thousand people of Japanese descent were incarcerated. Japanese American families had little time to sell their homes and businesses before being relocated to makeshift camps. Many families lost their property or sold their homes and businesses for far less money than they were worth. Japanese Americans were relocated to one of ten camps situated in western states away from the California coast. Housing was often livestock stalls. Camps were surrounded by barbed wire and guarded. Well-known photographer Ansel Adams took photos at the Manzanar War Relocation Center, one of the camps located in California. These photos can be viewed at "Ansel Adams's Photographs of Japanese-American Internment at Manzanar," Library of Congress, http://www.loc.gov/pictures/collection/manz.

Roosevelt not only called for the incarceration of Japanese Americans, but he also ordered Japanese Americans of draft age, not already fighting in the armed services, to be classified as 4-C, "enemy alien." This classification prohibited these young men from fighting for their country. When news of the racist treatment of Japanese Americans reached Japan, it confirmed for the Japanese the Pacific War was a just war against the United States and the West.

In 1943 Roosevelt reversed his draft order. Nearly 33,000 Japanese Americans volunteered to serve in the US armed forces, serving in combat roles and as interpreters and code breakers. The segregated Japanese American infantry unit the 442nd Infantry Regimental Combat Team fought in Europe and suffered 9,486 causalities there. The 442nd Regiment became the most decorated unit for its size and length of service in American history. For further information about the 442nd Regiment, see Yenne, *Rising Sons: The Japanese American GIs Who Fought for the United States in World War II.*

15: Bataan Death March: In April 1942, the Imperial Japanese Army forced some 60,000 to 80,000 Filipino and American prisoners of war (POWs) to make a 60-mile (97 km) walk with little food or water until they reached their prison destination. Many POWs were beaten or killed by their Japanese guards.

15: In Japan, racism generated its own brand of prejudice and hate: Dower, *Japan in War and Peace,* 271–279; Dower, *War without Mercy,* 203–261.

15: "Kill the American devil": Dower, *War without Mercy,* 248.

Imprisonment vs. internment: You won't find the term *internment* in this text. Legally, internment refers to confining noncitizens in a time of war. Because most Japanese Americans incarcerated during World War II were American citizens, I've instead used the terms *imprisonment* and *incarceration*. For more information, see "Euphemisms, Concentration Camps and the Japanese Internment," NPR Ombudsman, February 10, 2012, http://www.npr.org/sections/ombudsman/2012/02/10/146691773/euphemisms-concentration-camps-and-the-japanese-internment; National JACL Power of Words II Committee, "Power of Words Handbook: A Guide to Language About Japanese Americans in World War II," Japanese American Citizens League, April 27, 2013, https://jacl.org/wordpress/wp-content/uploads/2015/08/Power-of-Words-Rev.-Term.-Handbook.pdf.

EVACUATION

17: The Japanese government was drafting everyone who could fight: Ham, *Hiroshima Nagasaki,* 275–276.

Sachiko's family photographs: No photographs of Misa or Toshi were found.

"PROMPT AND UTTER DESTRUCTION"

20: Operation Downfall: If the Allies had invaded Japan, the invasion code-named Operation Downfall would have been the largest amphibious operation in history. The invasion plan was divided into two stages: Operation Olympic was scheduled for November 1945. American troops would attack the southern island of Kyushu, home to the city of Nagasaki. Operation Coronet would follow in March 1946 with Allied troops invading the Kanto Plain near Tokyo. The Japanese were aware of the Allies' plans. They prepared their own defensive operation named Ketsu-go, an all-out battle for their country.

21: Potsdam Conference: Complicated as the history may be, understanding events leading to the Potsdam Conference and the dire conditions in Japan are crucial to comprehending the decision to drop the atomic bomb. In addition to the events described in the text, other controversial issues played a role in the decision to drop the atomic bomb on Japan's cities.

Opinions within Truman's circle of advisers regarding the use of the bomb differed. When the topic of the atomic bomb came up, Assistant Secretary of War John McCloy argued that on moral grounds, the United States should warn Japan of the power of the atomic bomb and offer to retain the emperor under American occupation. James Byrnes, President Truman's newly sworn-in secretary of war, disagreed. In the end, Byrnes won the argument, although in the final Potsdam Declaration to the Japanese, the role of the emperor remained unclear. The Potsdam Declaration dictated the elimination "for all time of the authority and influence of those who have deceived and misled the people of Japan into embarking on world conquest," but it did not mention the emperor. Ham, *Hiroshima Nagasaki,* 198–199; "Potsdam Declaration," Atomic Archive, http://www.atomicarchive.com /Docs/Hiroshima/Potsdam.shtml.

Manhattan Project scientists working on the top-secret atomic bomb also differed in their opinions about using the weapon against Japan. Leading physicist Leo Szilard who, with Enrico Fermi, invented the nuclear reactor, questioned the dropping of the bomb. Szilard began a campaign to influence Truman. He suggested detonating the bomb on a deserted island to convince Japan to surrender. Szilard also argued that if the atomic bomb were used, it would ignite an arms race with the Soviet Union—a prediction that later came true. In a formal petition to Truman called the Franck Report, Szilard, James Franck, and a group of other like-minded atomic bomb scientists urged the president to rethink using the bomb on moral grounds. "The Franck Report," Atomic Heritage Foundation, http://www .atomicheritage.org/key-documents/franck-report.

21: "We call upon . . . prompt and utter destruction": "Potsdam Declaration," Atomic Archive, http://www.atomicarchive.com/Docs/Hiroshima/Potsdam.shtml.

21: The emperor's silence: Once Truman learned the atomic bomb test had been a success, he made up his mind to use the bomb if Japan did not unconditionally surrender. After the Allied leaders delivered the Potsdam Declaration on July 26, 1945, the Japanese government did not respond. In Japan the newly appointed prime minister, Kantaro Suzuki, gave a press conference during which he used the word *mokusatsu,* meaning "ignore" or "kill with silence." Whether this word was meant as a response to the Potsdam Declaration is still not clear. What is clear is that Truman interpreted the Japanese word *mokusatsu* and the silent response as a rejection of the Potsdam Declaration. The stage was set for disaster. "Mokusatsu: One Word, Two Lessons," National Security Agency, https://www.nsa.gov /public_info/_files/tech_journals/mokusatsu.pdf.

AN ORDINARY DAY

23: Yet another Japanese city struggling to survive: Collie, *Nagasaki,* 93–96; Frank, *Downfall,* 188–190; Southard, *Nagasaki,* 17–18.

Nagasaki's history: In the 1500s, the Portuguese sailed into Nagasaki harbor, bringing their Christian religion with them. Since Nagasaki was open to Western trade, the city became a center for Christianity and a wide range of religions were freely practiced. In 1635, Japan severed all ties with the West, and for a time a brutal anti-Christian campaign forced many Christians to go into hiding. Yet Nagasaki remained open to the West and continued to grow. By the late 1800s, Nagasaki was the seventh largest city in Japan. And by the 1920s, the Urakami Cathedral, the largest cathedral in the Far East, had been built. With the growth of the Mitsubishi Shipyard, Nagasaki became the third largest shipbuilding city in the world.

LITTLE BOY AND FAT MAN

26: Tibbets's flight: Ham, *Hiroshima Nagasaki,* 278–300.

27: "If [Japan's leaders] do not . . . on this earth": "Announcing the Bombing of Hiroshima," *American Experience,* http://www.pbs.org/wgbh/americanexperience/features/primary -resources/truman-hiroshima/.

The science of the atomic bomb: For information about atomic physics, nuclear fission, and the science behind Little Boy and Fat Man, see "Science," Atomic Archive, http://www.atomicarchive.com/sciencemenu.shtml; "Science Behind the Atom Bomb," Atomic Heritage Foundation, http://www.atomicheritage.org/history/science-behind-atom-bomb.

UNSPEAKABLE SECONDS

29–30: Sweeney's flight: Frank, *Downfall*, 283–284; Gordin, *Five Days in August*, 92–95; Southard, *Nagasaki*, 34–39.

31: "I got it! I got it": Southard, *Nagasaki*, 39.

THE END OF THE WORLD

33: An eerie, blinding light: "Overview," AtomicBombMuseum.org, http://atomicbombmuseum.org/1_overview.shtml.

33: Fires ignited everywhere: Nagai, ed., *Living Beneath the Atomic Cloud*, 15.

33: Ripped the bark off the camphor trees: Nagaskai Prefecture Teachers Association, *In the Sky over Nagasaki*, 14.

33: Not a house, not a tree stood: Nagai, ed., *Living Beneath the Atomic Cloud*, 29.

37: People shouted the names of relatives: Burke-Gaffney, trans., *The Light of Morning*, 7–8, 51.

37: People stumbled by, moaning. Some crawled on hands and knees: Burke-Gaffney, trans., *The Light of Morning*, 59.

MIZU

39: B-29 bombers continued to rumble overhead: Burke-Gaffney, trans., *The Light of Morning*, 9.

42: All dying for water: Lifton, *Death in Life*, 51.

"ENDURING THE UNENDURABLE"

44: The emperor's Supreme War Leadership Council bickered: Bix, *Hirohito and the Making of Modern Japan*, 525–530.

44: Broadcast of Hirohito's surrender speech: Bix, *Hirohito and the Making of Modern Japan*, 526–528; Burke-Gaffney, trans., *The Light of Morning*, 84; Lifton, *Death in Life*, 82–83.

44: "The war situation has developed . . . suffering what is insufferable": Hirohito, "Master Recording of Hirohito's War-End Speech Released in Digital Form," trans. Atsushi Kodera, *Japan Times*, August 1, 2015, http://www.japantimes.co.jp/news/2015/08/01/national/history/master-recording-hirohitos-war-end-speech-released-digital-form/#.Vw1OR2NhNFI.

45: "We must lay down our arms": Hogan, ed., *Hiroshima in History and Memory*, 1996, 114.

TWO BROTHERS

46: Ointment, Mercurochrome, or sometimes vegetable oil: Ham, *Hiroshima Nagasaki*, 414–415; Burke-Gaffney, trans., *The Light of Morning*, 12, 64.

49: "If I Go to the Sea" full lyrics: "Umi Yukaba," *Wikipedia*, February 15, 2016, https://en.wikipedia.org/wiki/Umi_Yukaba.

MIRACLE

50: Sachiko lay in bed: descriptions of radiation sickness in this paragraph are drawn from Burke-Gaffney, trans., *The Light of Morning*, 153.

RADIATION SICKNESS

52: Only 134 were within 0.6 miles (1,000 m) of the hypocenter: James Yamazaki states, "In the end, we were able to identify only 134 surviving children who had been within a thousand-meter radius, and only 12 who had been within five hundred meters": Yamazaki, *Children of the Atomic Bomb*, 85.

53: The scientists who had developed the atomic bomb were unaware of the effects of full-body radiation exposure: Southard, *Nagasaki*, 106–107.

Other victims of the bombs: Japanese living in Hiroshima and Nagasaki were not the only people who died or were injured as the result of the atomic bomb. Koreans, Chinese, and others who had been brought to Japan during the war as slave laborers and POWs were also killed or injured.

A NEW BEGINNING

54: Much of the city was still ash: "Life in the Ruins," AtomicBombMuseum.org, http://atomicbombmuseum.org/4_ruins.shtml.

56: "Women, stay on your guard . . . clumsy English": *Nagaski Shimbun,* September 14, 1945, quoted in Chad R. Diehl, "Resurrecting Nagasaki: Reconstruction, the Urakami Catholics, and Atomic Memory, 1945–1970" (PhD dissertation, Columbia University, 2011), http://hdl.handle.net/10022/AC:P:20900

57: "Ohio?" a soldier would say. "Oh heck, I'm from Indiana." Orval Amdahl, interview for the *Minnesota's Greatest Generation Oral History Project*, Part II, Minnesota History Center, January 10, 2006.

57: "Haro, haro": Nagai, *We of Nagasaki,* 20.

57: Soldiers giving children chocolate: Dower, *Embracing Defeat*, 110.

US servicemen and radiation exposure: Servicemen sent to Hiroshima and Nagasaki before 1946 were exposed to radiation levels that, for some, had long-term health effects. The unofficial term for veterans exposed to radiation is *atomic veterans*.

US OCCUPATION OF JAPAN

58: Changes in Japan after surrender: Dower, *Embracing Defeat*, 39–43; Southard, *Nagasaki,* 144–145; "The American Occupation of Japan, 1945–1952," Asia for Educators, http://afe.easia.columbia.edu/special/japan_1900_occupation.htm.

58: More than 240,000 American troops entered the country: Greg Mitchell, "The Last Great Untold Story of World War II—and the Lingering Effects Today," *Nation,* August 19, 2011, http://www.thenation.com/article/last-great-untold-story-world-war-ii-and-lingering-effects-today.

58: The destruction of Japan was nearly impossible to calculate: Dower, *Embracing Defeat*, 45, 50.

59: Article 9: Bix, *Hirohito and the Making of Modern Japan,* 569.

59: Legacy of Article 9: Since the early postwar years, Article 9 of Japan's constitution has remained controversial. Ironically, it was the United States that pressed for greater Japanese rearmament so that Japan could become a stronger military ally against the Soviet Union and China during the Cold War. The majority of Japanese people, devastated by war, supported their pacifist constitution and did not want to rearm. In September 2015, seventy years after World War II, Prime Minister Shinzo Abe pushed through a bill in the Japanese parliament (the Diet) to reinterpret Article 9. In a conservative shift in policy, Japan could now engage in overseas combat assignments under certain circumstances, defined as "collective self-defense." For further information about the controversial history of Article 9, see "Article 9 and the US–Japan Security Treaty," Asia for Educators, http://afe.easia .columbia.edu/special/japan_1950_usjapan.htm. For more information about Prime Minister Abe's redefinition of Article 9, see Matt Ford, "Japan Curtails Its Pacifist Stance," *Atlantic*, September 19, 2015, http://www.theatlantic.com/international/archive/2015/09 /japan-pacifism-article-nine/406318.

59: Hirohito's postwar role: Under the US occupation of Japan, Emperor Hirohito was to be transformed into a symbol of peace and democracy and deny his deity as a living god. See Dower, *Embracing Defeat*, 308–318.

SCHOOL

61: Changes to textbooks: Dower, *Embracing Defeat*, 246–251; Gordon, *A Modern History of Japan*, 229–230.

62: Censorship prevailed: Dower, *Embracing Defeat*, 406–414; Burke-Gaffney, trans., *The Light of Morning*, 41.

SEARCHING FOR HOPE

64: Effects of radiation on plants: The Committee for the Compilation of Materials on Damage Caused by the Atomic Bombs in Hiroshima and Nagasaki, *Hiroshima and Nagasaki*, 83–86.

A SEED FOR THE FUTURE

68: Coverage of Gandhi's death in Japan: *Mainichi Shimbun*, February 1, 1948.

69: "Nonviolence is the greatest force at the disposal of mankind": "Active Force," Mahatma Gandhi's Writings, Philosophy, Audio, Video, and Photographs, http://www.mkgandhi.org /nonviolence/phil2.htm.

STANDING UP TO THE BULLIES

73: Guilt of surviving the atomic bomb: Lifton, *Death in Life*, 37–56.

ANOTHER SEED FOR THE FUTURE

74: Helen Keller's 1948 visit to Nagasaki: "Tremendous Words for Nagasaki: We Welcomed Helen Keller and It Was impressive," *Nagasaki Shimbun*, October 17, 1948; "Helen and Polly visiting Japan 1948," video, available at American Foundation for the Blind, http://braillebug.afb.org /hkgallery.asp?frameid=42 (select video format below photograph on this page).

75: "Happy little bluebird . . . on Helen Keller's shoulder": "Blue Bird Song" by Hideyuki Iwahashi, quoted in "Tremendous Words for Nagasaki: We Welcomed Helen Keller and It Was Impressive," *Nagasaki Shimbun,* October 17, 1948.

76: Helen Keller cleared her throat and spoke to the thousands before her in a breathy voice, slowly, without changing pitch, sometimes garbled, but with great determination: "Helen Keller Speaks Out," *YouTube,* https://www.youtube.com/watch?v=8ch_H8pt9M8.

76: "May Nagasaki . . . was so damaged": "Tremendous Words for Nagasaki: We Welcomed Helen Keller and It Was Impressive," *Nagasaki Shimbun,* October 17, 1948.

76: Helen Keller's travels in Japan: Lash, *Helen and Teacher,* 642.

77: Helen Keller learning to speak: "1930 Rare Footage of Helen Keller Speaking with the Help of Anne Sullivan," *YouTube,* https://www.youtube.com/watch?v=GzlriQv16gg; "Helen Keller Speaks Out," *YouTube,* https://www.youtube.com/watch?v=8ch_H8pt9M8; Lash, *Helen and Teacher,* 114–115.

77: "Scorched a deep scar": Herrmann, *Helen Keller,* 293.

77: "I felt sure . . . smoke of death": Herrmann, *Helen Keller,* 294.

77: "against the demons of atomic warfare . . . and for peace": "Who's Helen Keller," *Teaching Tolerance* 24 (Fall 2003), http://www.tolerance.org/magazine/number-24-fall-2003/feature/whos-helen-keller.

More about Helen Keller in Nagasaki: While in Nagasaki, Helen Keller wished to meet the famous Dr. Takashi Nagai, also a survivor of the atomic bomb. Nagai had served as a medic in the Imperial Japanese Army in Manchuria and returned to Nagasaki to dedicate his life to radiology. Ironically, he had already been diagnosed with leukemia before the atomic bombing. Nagai's extraordinary efforts to help the wounded are described in his book *The Bells of Nagasaki.* Having converted to Christianity, Nagai's writing explored the meaning of great suffering, love, and forgiveness. The royalties from his publications supported projects to help the children of Nagasaki. Ill with leukemia, Nagai continued to write books while lying on his back in his small hut named Nyokodo, "Love Thy Neighbor as Thy Self." Considered the "Saint of Nagasaki" by many, Nagai died in 1951. He is buried at the Sakamoto International Cemetery. Sachiko Yasui knew of Nagai, but his writings were not influential in her own thinking. Her studies instead focused on her father's teachings and on the philosophy of nonviolence of Gandhi, Martin Luther King Jr., and others.

MISA AND THE ORPHANS OF WAR

78: Japan's economy during the Korean War: Dower, *Embracing Defeat,* 540–453; Gordon, *A Modern History of Japan,* 238–241.

78: Lives of Nagasaki orphans: Dower, *Embracing Defeat,* 61–64; "The Survivors," AtomicBombMuseum.org, http://atomicbombmuseum.org/4_survivors.shtml.

80: Many adults and children still suffered: The Committee for the Compilation of Materials on Damage Caused by the Atomic Bombs in Hiroshima and Nagasaki, *Hiroshima and Nagasaki,* 238; "Health Effects," AtomicBombMuseum.org, http://atomicbombmuseum.org/3_health.shtml; Yamazaki, *Children of the Atomic Bomb,* 114–115.

82: The *New Yorker* published an article: John Hersey's lengthy "Hiroshima" article was the only article in that issue of the *New Yorker*. The full article can be found here: John Hersey, "Hiroshima," *The New Yorker*, August 31, 1946, http://www.newyorker.com/magazine/1946/08/31/hiroshima.

82: *Harper's Magazine* article: Henry L. Stimson, "The Decision to Use the Atomic Bomb," *Harper's Magazine,* February 1947, https://inf2149decisionmaking.wikispaces.com/file/view/Stimson+-+Harper+Feb+1947+-+Decision+to+Use+the+Atomic+Bomb.pdf.

83: The Cold War also divided Asia: Another prominent Cold War division in Asia was the establishment of the People's Republic of China by Communist Mao Zedong in 1949. Nationalist leader Chiang Kai-shek, who had been a key member of the Allies during World War II, fled with his followers fled to Taiwan.

83: "I don't want to see it used. It is a terrible weapon": "The President's News Conference," Harry S. Truman Library and Museum, November 30, 1950, http://trumanlibrary.org/publicpapers/viewpapers.php?pid=985.

More about the events leading up to the Korean War: Although the Korean War was the first conflict of the Cold War, the seeds of the Cold War were planted even before the end of World War II. In February 1945, US president Franklin D. Roosevelt, British prime minister Winston Churchill, and the Soviet premier Joseph Stalin met at the Yalta Conference in the Soviet Union. The primary purpose of this meeting was to make plans for Germany's surrender and the reorganization of postwar Europe. At Yalta, Stalin agreed to enter the war against Japan within three months of Germany's surrender. As part of the agreement, the Soviet Union would regain territory lost to Japan in the Russo-Japanese War (1904–1905). Stalin also agreed to permit free elections in Eastern Europe but insisted that he control Eastern Europe as a defensive position. Stalin argued that Eastern Europe was within the Soviet Union's sphere of influence. After Yalta, Stalin was poised to swallow up Eastern Europe under his Communist umbrella, a move that would soon separate Eastern Europe from Western Europe with an "iron curtain" in between.

Korea had been discussed in 1943, when the leaders of Britain, the United States, and China met in Cairo, Egypt. In Cairo, Allied leaders decided Korea would be stripped away from Japan after Japan surrendered. The United States proposed that the Soviet Union would receive the surrender of Japan in Korea north of the 38th parallel. The Americans would receive the surrender of Japan south of the 38th parallel. The division between North and South Korea along the 38th parallel was viewed as a temporary administrative measure. As the Cold War intensified, the dividing line of the 38th parallel froze into place.

When the Korean War began, the United States saw the war as a Soviet Communist challenge to the free world. The United States decided to send troops to Korea under the umbrella of the United Nations. Eventually the Chinese army entered the war on the side of the Communists. The armistice in 1953 that ended the war did not reunify the two Koreas, but the agreement did avoid a potential nuclear war between the superpowers of the United States and the Soviet Union. Truman never expressed regret about the decision to drop the atomic bomb during World War II, but he did show signs of restraint during his 1950 press conference when he spoke about the horror of the atomic bomb.

FATHER

85: Hibakusha: Lifton, *Death in Life*, 7.

85: Keloids: Lifton, *Death in Life*, 172–174.

85: Hibakusha worries about marriage and children: Burke-Gaffney, trans., *The Light of Morning*, 96, 105; Lifton, *Death in Life*, 37–43; Yamazaki, *Children of the Atomic Bomb*, 122–123.

SACHIKO

88: Thyroid cancer rates: The Committee for the Compilation of Materials on Damage Caused by the Atomic Bombs in Hiroshima and Nagasaki, *Hiroshima and Nagasaki*, 276–277; Lifton, *Death in Life*, 104.

90: "The world is full of suffering . . . overcoming of it." Helen Keller, "My Future as I See It," document [source not identified], American Foundation for the Blind, http://www.afb.org /info/my-future-as-i-see-it-nd-document-source-not-identified/5.

91: "When one door . . . opened for us": Helen Keller, "We Bereaved," 1929, American Foundation for the Blind, http://www.afb.org/info/about-us/helen-keller/quotes/125.

LONG-TERM EFFECTS OF RADIATION

92: Eighteen percent higher risk of a leukemia diagnosis: Southard, *Nagasaki*, 177.

93: "We must wait . . . in succeeding generations:" Yamazaki, *Children of the Atomic Bomb*, 116–117.

Health care for hibakusha: A law was passed in Japan in 1957 to provide government health care for hibakusha. Many hibakusha found the initial application difficult to complete and the care inadequate for their needs. Hibakusha activists continued to work for better medical services. In 1995, an improved law went into effect.

More about James Yamazaki: Yamazaki was a young Japanese American pediatrician and World War II veteran assigned to lead the US Atomic Bomb Medical Team in Nagasaki after the war. His work in Nagasaki identified children who had been exposed to whole-body radiation, leading to greater understanding of thyroid cancer and leukemia in children. He was well aware that long-term studies were needed to understand the full impact of radiation exposure. Yamazaki continued to study the effects of radiation on children after the nuclear testing in the Bikini and Marshall Islands. He became an antinuclear activist and speaker as a result of his work. For a video of Dr. Yamazaki, see "Dr. James Yamazaki and the Children of the Atomic Bomb," YouTube, https://www.youtube.com /watch?v=ksmKUIhYMJs. For additional information about the long-term effects of radiation, see "The Survivors," AtomicBombMuseum.org, http://atomicbombmuseum.org /4_survivors.shtml.

ANOTHER WAY TO PEACE

94: "The only weapon that can save the world is nonviolence:" Dear introduction, *Mohandas Gandhi*, 145.

Note: The full quote from Gandhi is, "I hold that those who invented the atom bomb have committed the gravest sin in the world of science. The only weapon that can save the world is nonviolence. Considering the trend of the world, I might appear a fool to everyone. But I do not feel sorry for it. I rather consider it a great blessing that God did not make me capable of inventing the atom bomb." Dear introduction, *Mohandas Gandhi,* 145.

95: "I used to be very shy . . . poke fun at me": Gandhi, *Autobiography,* 4.

97: "Love is a skill . . . can be learned": Fischer, *The Essential Gandhi,* xxvi.

97: "Nonviolence is not a garment to be put on and off at will": Dear introduction, *Mohandas Gandhi,* 110.

"THE WORLD HOUSE"

100: "I have a dream . . . ": King, "I Have a Dream" speech, 1963.

100: "At the center of nonviolence stands the principle of love": King, *A Testament of Hope,* 19.

100: "Darkness cannot . . . only love can do that": King, *Strength to Love,* 53.

101: "The large house in which . . . a world-wide brotherhood": King, "The World House," quoted in King, *"In a Single Garment of Destiny,"* 12.

101: "Our lives begin . . . things that matter": King, Sermon delivered in Selma, Alabama, on March 8, 1965.

THE H-BOMB

102: Nuclear arsenal statistics: "Historical Nuclear Weapons Stockpiles and Nuclear Tests by Country," *Wikipedia,* March 25, 2016, https://en.wikipedia.org/wiki/Historical_nuclear_weapons_stockpiles_and_nuclear_tests_by_country.

103: Anti-nuclear protests in Japan: In response to the *Lucky Dragon #5* incident, 32 million Japanese people signed a petition against the hydrogen bomb. To commemorate the tenth anniversary of the atomic bombings in 1955, The First World Conference Against Atomic and Hydrogen Bombs was organized in Hiroshima. Approximately thirty thousand people attended the conference at the Hiroshima Memorial Peace Park. Southard, *Nagaksaki,* 212.

More about the Cold War and nuclear weapons: As the Japanese struggled to recover from the destruction of World War II and the atomic bombings, Americans looked toward the future with both dread and optimism. The Atomic Age was a time of great anxiety as competition increased for nuclear weapons, particularly between the United States and the Soviet Union. In an effort to protect the public, the US government established civil defense procedures all over the country. Towns and cities built fallout shelters. Citizens built private bomb shelters, and schoolchildren hid under their desks for "duck and cover" drills in case of a nuclear attack. On the bright side, many Americans viewed nuclear energy as a major technological breakthrough. In the future, nuclear energy would power everything necessary for clean, modern living. During the Cold War, fear and hope went hand in hand.

As the Cold War intensified, the United States and the Soviet Union came to the brink of nuclear war. In 1962 the United States detected nuclear-armed Soviet missiles in the newly Communist island-state of Cuba, only 90 miles (145 km) off the coast of Florida. These missiles were in striking distance of nearly every major US city. Americans faced possible nuclear destruction of their own country. For thirteen days, US president John F. Kennedy and Soviet premier Nikita Khrushchev negotiated over the removal of the Cuban missiles. What did Sachiko Yasui think of the Cuban Missile Crisis? "It was a good lesson for the world."

By 1970 the United States and the Soviet Union were working together to find ways to control the nuclear arms race. The Treaty on the Non-Proliferation of Nuclear Weapons (NPT) was the result. The NPT is considered the most significant and successful treaty to eliminate nuclear weapons. According to the treaty's terms, the five countries already possessing nuclear arsenals—the United States, the Soviet Union, China, France, and Britain—can continue to possess nuclear arms but must make long-term commitments to disarm as well as share the benefits of nuclear technology for peaceful purposes. All other nations agreeing to the treaty are to renounce or reduce their nuclear arms program. In 1995 the treaty was extended indefinitely and is reviewed every five years.

To date, the United States, Russia (formerly the Soviet Union), the United Kingdom, France, and China have signed the NPT to end the spread of nuclear arms. India first tested a nuclear weapon in 1974, Pakistan in 1998, and North Korea in 2006, but none of these countries have signed the NPT. Israel is believed to have nuclear weapons but has refused to state its capability.

For more information about nuclear disarmament and the NPT, see "Treaty on the Non-Proliferation of Nuclear Weapons (NPT)," United Nations Office for Disarmament Affairs, http://www.un.org/disarmament/WMD/Nuclear/NPT.shtml. For a nuclear weapons timeline, see "Nuclear Weapons Timeline," International Campaign to Abolish Nuclear Weapons, http://www.icanw.org/the-facts/the-nuclear-age.

For more on new nuclear weapons development in 2016, see William J. Broad and David E. Sanger, "Race for Latest Class of Nuclear Arms Threatens to Revive Cold War," *New York Times*, April 16, 2016, http://www.nytimes.com/2016/04/17/science/atom-bomb-nuclear-weapons-hgv-arms-race-russia-china.html.

CICADA YEARS

104: Cicada nymphs: "Cicada," *National Geographic Kids,* http://kids.nationalgeographic.com/animals/cicada.

106: Hirohito's death: Susan Chira, "Hirohito, 124th Emperor of Japan, Is Dead at 87," *New York Times*, January 7, 1989.

106: End of the Cold War: Scholars do not agree on why the Cold War ended. Some hold that US military strength under President Reagan forced the Soviet Union into bankruptcy as it tried to keep up in the arms race. Others argue that the Soviet Union imploded because of the weaknesses of its government and had little to do with external pressures. Some scholars believe the Soviet Union would have collapsed even earlier if it had not been for the propaganda of the Cold War. Pointing to the United States as the hated enemy may even have helped the Soviet Union strengthen the legitimacy of its government in the eyes of its people.

107: "You must be the change you wish to see in the world": This quote is attributed to Gandhi, "Quotes," The Official Mahatma Gandhi eArchive & Reference Library, http://www.mahatma.org.in/mahatma/quotes/quotes.jsp?link=qt.

THE FIFTIETH ANNIVERSARY

108: Shooting of Mayor Hitoshi Motoshima: Southard, *Nagasaki*, 258; David Sanger, "Mayor Who Faulted Hirohito Is Shot," *New York Times,* January 19, 1990.

109: In the United States, emotions ran high as well: Lifton and Mitchell, *Hiroshima in America*, 276–279, 295–297.

109: Smithsonian exhibit: Kilian, "Smithsonian Gives In, Cancels A-bomb Exhibit," *Chicago Tribune*, January 31, 1995, http://articles.chicagotribune.com/1995-01-31/news/9501310181_1_important-anniversary-year-enola-gay-michael-heyman. A PDF of the original exhibition script can be found at "The Last Act: The Atomic Bomb and the End of World War II," ERIC, http://eric.ed.gov/?id=ED401218.

More controversy in the United States: To commemorate the fiftieth anniversary of the atomic bombing, the US Postal Service planned to issue a stamp featuring the atomic mushroom cloud. The stamp's caption read: "Atomic bombs hasten war's end, August 1945." The mayor of Nagasaki, Hitoshi Motoshima, called the stamp "heartless." The Japanese Embassy asked the US government to reconsider issuing the stamp, and the stamp was ultimately replaced with a depiction of President Truman. For more information, see Andrew Pollack, "Japan Protests U.S. Stamp on A-Bomb," *New York Times*, December 4, 1994, http://www.nytimes.com/1994/12/04/world/japan-protests-us-stamp-on-a-bombs.html; Trupti Rami, "Return to Sender," *New York Magazine*, December 1, 2013, http://nymag.com/news/intelligencer/us-stamp-controversy-2013-12.

SACHIKO'S FIFTH ANNIVERSARY

This chapter weaves together interview notes and Sachiko's classroom presentations. Below are additional quotes Sachiko has shared with students in Japan:

"We hope to be healthy and live long. We hope to accomplish something using our inborn talent while we're alive. We hope not to be looked down on by others. These are our most basic wishes as human beings. We hope to live in peace without discrimination."

"I believe these are our common wishes, our fundamental human rights. The atomic bomb that destroyed Nagasaki was what trampled those human rights. It impaired our dignity. This kind of story cannot resonate in your heart unless your mind is open and full of sensitivity."

"War makes the biggest discrimination in our lives. Discrimination deprives us of our lives, our hometown, our pride, our jobs, our abilities. . . . Before we learn the tragedy of wars and atomic bombs, we must abolish discrimination in our daily lives. Let us be brave together."

"I am very happy to feel how important speaking is again. People cannot convey peace to the world until they get over their personal sorrow and pain. I overcame mine. It is natural that I talk to young people in the world for their future."

"You need to lead your heart to peace. Plant peace in your heart. Then try to change someone else's heart. One small string tied to one small string. One person to one person. Group by group. Country to country. We are all connected."

"Choose your path wisely and follow it. You do not have to do big things. Do small things, little by little. If you are having a hard time, remember me."

AUTHOR'S NOTE

116: "No one denies . . . on Japanese cities": John W. Dower, "Triumphal and Tragic Narratives of the War in Asia," *The Journal of American History*, Vol. 82, No. 3 (Dec., 1995), pp. 1124–1135, http://www.jstor.org/stable/2945119.

ACKNOWLEDGMENTS

Sachiko's story is written through the lenses of memory, translation, interpretation, and conjecture. I am acutely aware of the fallibility of these lenses. Where I have made errors in fact or presumption, I am responsible. Where I have been successful, I owe to all who have helped me.

Many thanks go to my Nagasaki friends. First, heartfelt thanks goes to Takayuki Miyanishi, professor of environmental science at Nagasaki University and president of the Nagasaki–Saint Paul Sister City Committee, who provided hours of translation time, recording equipment, and commitment to this story. Takayuki-san is the hero of this project. I'd also like to thank Fumiko Yamaguchi, vice president of the Nagasaki–Saint Paul Sister City Committee, for her help coordinating my visits to Nagasaki and help communicating with Sachiko. Thanks also to Chizuko Miyazaki of the Nagasaki–Saint Paul Sister City Committee for her help, Yasushi Oba at the Atomic Bomb Museum for resources, and to Etsuko Matsuo for her friendship and intimate reminisces. Great thanks goes to Tadahiro Motomura, past president of the Nagasaki newspaper, for helping me peer into the archives of the *Nagasaki Shimbun*. I am also grateful to Hiroyuki and Keiko Kawase of Hiroshima for the 2012 scholarship to the Hiroshima City University Peace Forum. Of course, I am indebted to Sachiko Yasui for her friendship and her trust in me to write her story. *Domo arigato gozaimasu* to all.

Sachiko could not have been written without my Minnesota friends and colleagues who supported this project from its inception. Hearty thanks go to JoAnn Blatchley, longtime friend and president of the Saint Paul–Nagasaki Sister City Committee and Fusako Mora, who translated my first letter to Sachiko. My greatest thanks goes to Keiko Kawakami, teaching specialist of Japanese at the University of Minnesota, faithful translator, and friend, who stayed with me throughout this project. Without Keiko, I would have been lost.

Research and accuracy were critical to the writing of this manuscript. Many thanks go to the following who generously offered their time and subject matter expertise: Hiromi Mizuno, professor of Japanese history at the University of Minnesota; Sumiko Otsubo, professor of history at Metropolitan State University; Timothy W. Beck, professor of physics, astronomy, and engineering at Mendocino College; reader Kumi Mizuno; Helen Seldon, archivist at the American Foundation for the Blind in New York City; Walter Enloe, professor of education at Hamline University, Saint Paul, Minnesota, and former teacher and principal at Hiroshima International School, Hiroshima; and Steve Leeper, former director of the Hiroshima Peace Museum and Cultural Center and specialist in Gandhi's influence in Japan.

For insight into the experience of the World War II American soldier, I interviewed Orval Amdahl, former Marine captain, who shared his experiences fighting in the Pacific War and his memories of Nagasaki as part of the occupying force. During that year of interviews, we successfully returned Mr. Amdahl's "war souvenir," a Japanese sword, to the Motomura family of Nagasaki, the sword's original owners. I also would like to thank Clifton Truman Daniel, the eldest grandson of President Harry Truman, for our discussions about the difficult history surrounding the dropping of the atomic bombs and the process of peace and reconciliation.

Nagasaki's One-Legged Torii Gate in 2012

Researching a book takes one community, writing a book takes another. Heartfelt thanks go to my extraordinary circle of writing friends and colleagues: Jane Resh Thomas, author, editor, and writing mentor; Kristin Gallagher, Laurie Johnson, and the Muskrat Writing Group; author Phyllis Root; and Elizabeth Partridge my mentor at the Highlights Workshop for Narrative Nonfiction in Honesdale, Pennsylvania. Appreciation goes to the Society of Children's Book Writers and Illustrators for the generous Anna Cross Giblin Award for a nonfiction work-in-progress in 2013.

I am grateful to all who supported the writing of *Sachiko* as a manuscript, but *Sachiko* would never have emerged as a book without the care and guidance of Rubin Pfeffer, literary agent, and Carol Hinz, editor extraordinaire at Carolrhoda Books/Lerner Publishing Group.

Lastly, I thank my patient husband, Kim, who, at the beginning of my Sachiko journey, asked me, "Do you *need* to go to Nagasaki?"

BIBLIOGRAPHY

This list includes all the books I consulted as well as key articles and speeches. The most informative websites are mentioned in the notes section or on the resources page. Sources marked with an asterisk (*) were particularly useful in researching this book.

PUBLISHED MATERIAL BY AND ABOUT SACHIKO YASUI

Esaki, Ken'ichi. "Sachiko Yasui Interviews." *Asahi Shimbun*, September 4–11, 2011.

Yasui, Sachiko. "Contribute Actively to Peace." Speech delivered at Nagasaki University. Video (December 1, 2011). http://naosite.lb.nagasaki-u.ac.jp/dspace/handle/10069/28510. Link to PDF of English transcript (March 31, 2013). http://naosite.lb.nagasaki-u.ac.jp/dspace/handle /10069/33737.
A note about the speech and transcript: The transcript available offers a few details that are different from those I learned through my interviews with Sachiko. These differences may be the result of retelling, translation, or my decisions as a writer.

———. "The Experiences of My Family in the Atomic Bombing." Ministry of Foreign Affairs of Japan. Accessed April 21, 2016. http://www.mofa.go.jp/policy/un/disarmament/arms /testimony_of_hibakusha/pdfs/10e.pdf.

———. "That Day: Handing Down My Experience of Radiation Exposure." *Southwestern Japan Newspaper*, August 9, 2005.

WORLD WAR II AND THE PACIFIC WAR

Benedict, Ruth. *The Chrysanthemum and the Sword: Patterns of Japanese Culture*. Boston: Houghton Mifflin Company, 1946.
A note about this source: This book was commissioned by the US government during World War II out of a desire to better understand Japanese culture. Benedict, an anthropologist, could not go to Japan for her research because of the war, so she interviewed Japanese Americans in the United States. Her book is an interesting piece of war history as well as a resource, although questionable.

*Bix, Herbert P. *Hirohito and the Making of Modern Japan*. New York: HarperCollins, 2000.

Chira, Susan. "Hirohito, 124th Emperor of Japan, Is Dead at 87." *New York Times*, January 7, 1989.

*Cirincione, Joseph. *Bomb Scare: The History and Future of Nuclear Weapons*. New York: Columbia University Press, 2007

*Collie, Craig. *Nagasaki: The Massacre of the Innocent and Unknowing*. Crows Nest, NSW: Allen & Unwin, 2011.

*Collingham, Lizzie. *The Taste of War: World War II and the Battle for Food*. New York: Penguin, 2012.

*The Committee for the Compilation of Materials on Damage Caused by the Atomic Bombs in Hiroshima and Nagasaki. *Hiroshima and Nagasaki: The Physical, Medical, Social Effects of the Atomic Bombings*. Translated by Eisei Ishikawa and David L. Swain. New York: Basic Books, 1981.

Diehl, Chad, trans. *And the River Flowed as a Raft of Corpses: The Poetry of Yamaguchi Tsutomu, Survivor of both Hiroshima and Nagasaki*. New York: Excogitating over Coffee, 2010.

———. "Resurrecting Nagasaki: Reconstruction, the Urakami Catholics, and Atomic Memory, 1945–1970." PhD diss., Columbia University, 2011. http://hdl.handle.net/10022/AC:P:20900.

*Dower, John W. *Embracing Defeat: Japan in the Wake of World War II*. New York: W. W. Norton, 1999.

*———. *Japan in War and Peace: Selected Essays.* New York: New Press, 1993.

*———. *War without Mercy: Race and Power in the Pacific War.* New York: Pantheon Books, 1986.

Enloe, Walter. *Lessons from Ground Zero: A Hiroshima and Nagasaki Story.* St. Paul: Hamline University Press, 2002.

*Frank, Richard B. *Downfall: The End of the Imperial Japanese Empire.* New York: Random House, 1999.

Goldstein, Donald, M., Katherine V. Dillon, and J. Michael Wenger. *Rain of Ruin: A Photographic History of Hiroshima and Nagasaki.* Washington: Brassey's, 1995.

*Gordin, Michael D. *Five Days in August: How World War II Became a Nuclear War.* Princeton, NJ: Princeton University Press, 2007.

*Gordon, Andrew. *A Modern History of Japan: From Tokugawa Times to the Present.* 2nd ed. New York: Oxford University Press, 2009.

*Ham, Paul. *Hiroshima Nagasaki: The Real Story of the Atomic Bombings and Their Aftermath.* New York: Thomas Dunne Books, 2011.

Hersey, John. *Hiroshima.* New York: A. A. Knopf, 1946.

Hogan, Michael J., ed. *Hiroshima in History and Memory.* Cambridge, UK: Cambridge University Press, 1996.

Jenkins, Rupert, ed. *Nagasaki Journey: The Photographs of Yosuke Yamahata, August 10, 1945.* San Francisco: Pomegranate Artbooks, 1995.

Kakehashi, Kumiko. *So Sad to Fall in Battle: An Account of War.* New York: Presidio Press, 2007.

Kilian, Michael, "Smithsonian Gives in, Cancels A-Bomb Exhibit." *Chicago Tribune,* January 31, 1995.

Lifton, Betty Jean. *A Place Called Hiroshima.* Tokyo: Kodansha, 1985.

*Lifton, Robert J. *Death in Life: Survivors of Hiroshima.* New York: Random House, 1967.

*Lifton, Robert Jay, and Greg Mitchell. *Hiroshima in America: Fifty Years of Denial.* New York: Putnam's Sons, 1995.

Matsubara, Hiroshi. "Interview: Ex-Nagasaki Mayor Motoshima: Nuclear-Free Japan a 'Matter of Course'?" *Ashai Shimbun,* August 9, 2012.

Nasu, Masamoto. *Hiroshima: A Tragedy Never to Be Repeated.* English ed. English text by Joanna King and Toshiyuki Tanaka. Tokyo: Fukuinkan Shoten, 1998.

Nobuaki, Nakagawa. "Terror, Taboo, and Silence: Speaking Out on the Emperor System." *AMPO: Japan-Asia Quarterly Review* 21, no. 4 (1990): 57–58.

*Reeves, Richard. *Infamy: The Shocking Story of the Japanese American Internment in World War II.* New York: Henry Holt, 2015.

Sanger, David E. "Mayor Who Faulted Hirohito Is Shot." *New York Times,* January 19, 1990. http://www.nytimes.com/1990/01/19/world/mayor-who-faulted-hirohito-is-shot.html.

Schwartz, Stephen I. "The Hidden Costs of Our Nuclear Arsenal." The Brookings Institution. June 30, 1998. http://www.brookings.edu/about/projects/archive/nucweapons/schwartz.

Siracusa, Joseph M. *Nuclear Weapons: A Very Short Introduction.* 2nd ed. Oxford: Oxford University Press, 2015.

*Southard, Susan. *Nagasaki: Life after Nuclear War.* New York: Viking, 2015.

Sweeney, Charles W. *War's End: An Eyewitness Account of America's Last Atomic Mission.* With James A. Antonucci and Marion K. Antonucci. New York: Avon Books, 1997.

*Yamazaki, James N. *Children of the Atomic Bomb: An American Physician's Memoir of Nagasaki, Hiroshima, and the Marshall Islands.* With Louis B. Fleming. Durham, NC: Duke University Press, 1995.

Yenne, Bill. *Rising Sons: The Japanese American GIs Who Fought for the United States in World War II.* New York: Thomas Dunne Books, 2007.

HIROSHIMA/NAGASAKI: ORAL HISTORY

*Amdahl, Orval. Interviewed for "Minnesota's Greatest Generation Oral History Project: Part II." Minnesota History Center, January 10, 2006.

*Burke-Gaffney, Brian, trans. *The Light of Morning: Memoirs of the Nagasaki Atomic Bomb Survivors.* Nagasaki: Nagasaki National Peace Memorial Hall for the Atomic Bomb Victims, 2005.

Cook, Haruko Taya, and Theodore F. Cook. *Japan at War: An Oral History.* New York: New Press, 1992.

Nagasaki Prefecture Hibakusha Teachers Association. *In the Sky over Nagasaki: An A-Bomb Reader for Children.* Translated by Cheryl Green Lammers. Wilmington, OH: Wilmington College, 1983.

*Nagasaki Testimonial Society Century. *Voices of the A-Bomb Survivors: Nagasaki.* Nagasaki: Nagasaki Testimonial Society Century, 2009.

Nakano, Michiko, ed. *Nagasaki under the Atomic Bomb: Experiences of Young College Girls.* Tokyo: Soeisha/Hatsubai Sanseido Shoten, 2000.

*Selden, Kyoko, and Mark Selden, eds. *The Atomic Bomb: Voices from Hiroshima and Nagasaki.* Armonk, NY: M. E. Sharpe, 1989.

TAKASHI NAGAI

Glynn, Paul. *A Song for Nagasaki: The Story of Takashi Nagai, Scientist, Convert and Survivor of the Atomic Bomb.* San Francisco: Ignatius, 2009.

*Nagai, Takashi. *The Bells of Nagasaki.* Translated by William Johnston. New York: Distributed through Harper & Row, 1984. Originally published as *Nagasaki no Kane* (Tokyo: Kodansha, 1984).

———. *Leaving My Beloved Children Behind.* Translated by Maurice M. Tatsuoka and Takai Tsuneyoshi. Staten Island, NY: St. Paul's Publications, 2008.

———, ed. *Living Beneath the Atomic Cloud: Testimony of Children of Nagasaki.* Compiled by Frank Zenisek. Nagaski: Nagasaki Appeal Committee, 1979.

*———. *We of Nagasaki: The Story of Survivors in an Atomic Wasteland.* Translated by Ichiro Shirato and Herbert B. L. Silverman. New York: Duell, Sloan and Pearce, 1951.

HELEN KELLER

*"Helen Keller: Our Champion." American Foundation for the Blind. Accessed April 21, 2016. http://www.afb.org/info/about-us/helen-keller/12.

*Herrmann, Dorothy. *Helen Keller: A Life.* New York: A. Knopf, 1998.

Keller, Helen. *The Story of My Life: The Complete and Unabridged Edition.* Seven Treasures Publication, 2008.

*Lash, Joseph P. *Helen and Teacher: The Story of Helen Keller and Anne Sullivan Macy*. New York: Delacorte, 1980.

"Our History." Nippon Lighthouse: Welfare Center for the Blind. Accessed April 21, 2016. http://www.lighthouse.or.jp/rekisi_e.html.

"Takeo Iwahashi." Nippon Lighthouse: Welfare Center for the Blind. Accessed April 21, 2016. http://www.lighthouse.or.jp/takeo_e.html.

"We Welcomed Helen Keller and It Was Impressive." *Nagasaki Shimbun*, October 17, 1948.

MOHANDAS K. GANDHI

Andrews, Charles, F. *Mahatama Gandhi: His Life and Ideas*. Woodstock, VT: SkyLight Paths, 2003.

*Fischer, Louis. *Gandhi: His Life and Message for the World*. New York: Signet Classics, 1982.

Gandhi, Mahatma. *The Essential Gandhi: An Anthology of His Writings on His Life, Work, and Ideas*. 2nd ed. Edited by Louis Fischer. New York: Vintage Books, 2002.

*————. *Mohandas Gandhi: Essential Writings*. Selected with an introduction by John Dear. Maryknoll, NY: Orbis Books, 2002.

*Gandhi, Mohandas K. *Autobiography: The Story of My Experiments with Truth*. New York: Dover Publications, 1983.

Leeper, Steve. *Hiroshima Revolution*. Atlanta: Global Peacemakers Association, 2004.

Merton, Thomas, ed. *Gandhi on Nonviolence*. New York: New Directions, 1965.

MARTIN LUTHER KING JR.

*Dudziak, Mary L. "The Global March on Washington." *New York Times*, August 27, 2013. http://www.nytimes.com/2013/08/28/opinion/the-global-march-on-washington.html.

Kakutani, Michiko. "The Lasting Power of Dr. King's Dream Speech." *New York Times*, August 27, 2013. http://www.nytimes.com/2013/08/28/us/the-lasting-power-of-dr-kings-dream-speech.html.

*King, Martin Luther, Jr. *The Autobiography of Martin Luther King*. Edited by Clayborne Carson. New York: Intellectual Properties Management / Warner Books, 1998.

————. *A Call to Conscience: The Landmark Speeches of Dr. Martin Luther King, Jr.* Edited by Clayborne Carson and Kris Shepard. New York: Intellectual Properties Management / Warner Books, 2001.

*————. *I Have a Dream: Writing and Speeches That Changed the World*. Edited by James Melvin Washington. New York: HarperCollins, 1986.

*————. *"In a Single Garment of Destiny": A Global Vision of Justice*. Edited by Lewis V. Baldwin. Boston: Beacon, 2012.

————. *A Testament of Hope: The Essential Writings of Martin Luther King, Jr.* Edited by James Melvin Washington. San Francisco: HarperSanFrancisco, 1991.

————. *Strength to Love*. Philadelphia: Fortress Press, 1981.

————. *Why We Can't Wait*. New York: Harper & Row, 1964.

RESOURCES

Many resources are available about World War II and the Pacific War; the atomic bombings of Hiroshima and Nagasaki; the nuclear arms race; and the study of peace, reconciliation, and nuclear disarmament. Below is a short list of sources not cited in the bibliography or notes that are particularly relevant:

BOOKS

Coerr, Eleanor. *Sadako and the Thousand Paper Cranes.* New York: Putnam, 1977.

Hillenbrand, Laura. *Unbroken: An Olympian's Journey from Airman to Castaway to Captive.* (The Young Adult Adaptation.) New York: Delacorte, 2014.

Ibuse, Masuji. *Black Rain.* Translated by John Bester. Tokyo: Kodansha, 1969.

Nagai, Mariko. *Dust of Eden.* Chicago: Albert Whitman, 2014.

Park, Linda Sue. *When My Name Was Keoko.* New York: Clarion Books, 2002.

Sheinkin, Steve. *Bomb: The Race to Build—and Steal—the World's Most Dangerous Weapon.* New York: Roaring Brook, 2012.

WEBSITES

Children of the Atomic Bomb
> http://www.aasc.ucla.edu/cab/index.html
> This site, created by Dr. James N. Yamazaki together with the UCLA Asian American Studies Center, offers information about Yamazaki as well as lesson plans and other resources.

Disarmament Education
> http://www.un.org/disarmament/education/index.html
> The United Nations Office for Disarmament Affairs provides a range of resources related to peace and disarmament, including reports, articles, podcasts, films, and links.

Harry S. Truman Library and Museum: The Decision to Drop the Atomic Bomb
> http://www.trumanlibrary.org/whistlestop/study_collections/bomb/large/index.php
> The Harry S. Truman Library and Museum offers primary source documents as well as photographs and oral histories related to the atomic bombings of Hiroshima and Nagasaki.

Hibakusha Stories
> http://www.hibakushastories.org
> This site provides resources, hibakusha testimonials, and more about the atomic bombings of Hiroshima and Nagasaki.

Nuclear Zero
> http://nuclearzero.org
> This site, which has information about the Marshall Islands, the site of many US nuclear tests, includes an interactive tool called Nukemap. Scroll to the bottom of the main page to find this nuclear simulation. Options include selecting the city and size of bomb, which allows users to envision what might happen if a nuclear bomb exploded over their city.

"1945–1998"
> http://www.ctbto.org/specials/1945-1998-by-isao-hashimoto/
> Created by Japanese artist Isao Hashimoto, this video shows a time-lapse representation of nuclear explosions worldwide from 1945 to 1998.

INDEX

PHOTO ACKNOWLEDGMENTS

The images in this book are used with the permission of: © iStockphoto.com/chuyu (silhouetted tree); © Design56/Dreamstime.com, p. 1; © Laura Westlund/Independent Picture Service, pp. 4, 21 (top), 25, 53; © Danielle Carnito, p. 6; © AFP/Getty Images, pp. 11, 13; © Stocktrek Images, Inc./Alamy, p. 12; The Granger Collection, New York, pp. 14, 17, 32; © Galerie Bilderwelt/ Hulton Archive/Getty Images, p. 15 (top); © Universal History Archive/UIG/Getty Images, p. 15 (bottom); © Bettman/Corbis, p. 21 (bottom left); Harry S. Truman Library, p. 21 (bottom right); © Hulton Archive/Getty Images, p. 22; Public Domain, p. 22; © Universal History Archive/Getty Images, p. 25; © Corbis, pp. 27 (all), 92; © Everett Collection Inc/Alamy, pp. 30, 34; © Photo Researchers/Alamy, p. 37; © Galerie Bilderwelt/Hulton Archive/Getty Images, p. 40; AP Photo, pp. 41, 79; © INTERFOTO/Alamy, pp. 44, 105; AP Photo/Kyodo, p. 45; © Yasuo Tomishige/The Asahi Shimbun/Getty Images, pp. 47, 48; © Ryszard Stelmachowicz/Alamy, p. 51; © SuperStock, p. 52; AP Photo/ACME, p. 55; © Roger Viollet/Getty Images, p. 56; © Popperfoto/Getty Images, p. 58; © Keystone/Hulton Royals Collection/Getty Images, p. 59; © Nagasaki Atomic Bomb Museum, pp. 62, 65; © Rühe/ullstein bild/Getty Images, p. 68; © Yasuo Tomishige/The Asahi Shimbun/Getty Images, p. 73; © Time Life Pictures/Pix Inc./The LIFE Picture Collection/Getty Images, p. 76; © Alfred Eisenstaedt/Pix Inc./The LIFE Picture Collection/Getty Images, p. 80; National Archives (541959), p. 83; © AWL Images RM/Getty Images, p. 85; © Gary Friedman/ Los Angeles Times/Getty Images, p. 93; © Houjyou-Minori/Wikimedia Commons (CC BY-SA 3.0 US), p. 95; © Dinodia Photos/Alamy, p. 96; © Michael Ochs Archives/Getty Images, p. 99; © Central Press/Hulton Archive/Getty Images, p. 100; © Galerie Bilderwelt/Hulton Archive/ Getty Images, p. 103; CSU Archives/Everett Collection/Newscom, p. 104; © Mitsuhiko Imamori/ Minden Pictures, p. 106; © imageBROKER/Alamy, p. 108; © FourT4/Alamy, p. 109; Courtesy of the author, pp. 114, 135.

Family photos: Courtesy of Sachiko Yasui.

Front cover: Courtesy of Sachiko Yasui (girl); © Design56/Dreamstime.com (orange treatment). Back cover: © Everett Collection Inc/Alamy.